Southern Biscuits

Southern Biscuits

NATHALIE DUPREE

and

CYNTHIA GRAUBART

PHOTOGRAPHS *by* RICK McKEE

GIBBS SMITH
TO ENRICH AND INSPIRE HUMANKIND

First Edition
11 12 13 14 15   5 4 3 2 1

Published by
Gibbs Smith
P.O. Box 667
Layton, Utah 84041

1.800.835.4993 orders
www.gibbs-smith.com

Designed and produced by Michelle Farinella Design
Printed and bound in Hong Kong
Gibbs Smith books are printed on paper produced from sustainable
PEFC-certified forest/controlled wood source.
Learn more at www.pefc.org.

Library of Congress Cataloging-in-Publication Data

Dupree, Nathalie, author.
Southern biscuits / Nathalie Dupree and Cynthia Stevens Graubart ;
Photographs by Rick McKee. — First edition.
p. cm.
Includes bibliographical references and index.
ISBN 978-1-4236-2176-8
1. Biscuits. 2. Cooking, American—Southern style.
I. Graubart, Cynthia Stevens, author. II. Title.
TX770.B55D86 2011
641.8'15—dc22
                            2010042659

To the Dupree-Bass Family and the Graubart Family
And with thanks to all our
biscuit-making friends who helped so much.

—Nathalie and Cynthia

Contents

Tomorrow's Biscuits

Gilding the Lily

Desserts

Acknowledgments

Where to start with our acknowledgements? First, of course, our families, which are a bit intertwined as Cynthia was my producer for *New Southern Cooking* when she was a young woman. I introduced her to her husband, Cliff Graubart, stood up for her at her wedding in Rome, and have watched her beautiful wise children, Rachel and Norman, grow up. Cliff was the first friend of mine to meet my husband, Jack Bass, a minute after I did. He thought we were already an item. Our families have put up with our traveling back and forth between Atlanta and Charleston to work together, hours on the computer, dozens—hundreds—thousands of biscuits coming out of the oven and going into various concoctions, some successful, some not, which they dutifully ate. Rachel Graubart and my husband Jack Bass' granddaughter, who I claim too, and Rachel Bass tested recipes for us. Norman Graubart, a literalist, tested recipes for us and brought us new insights to our detailed recipe instructions.

The most important person after our families is Deidre Schipanni. Deidre—a multifaceted person with many years of training in science and other degrees she holds, professional cooking, writing, testing recipes, and writing—helped me for several years, including some of the science information for biscuits. We are truly grateful for her wisdom and many hours of effort on our behalf.

Thank you to our wonderful photographer, Rick McKee, and all the others who worked on this book. There were many interns, paid assistants, and many students who have studied with me, who worked one by one on this book—we are grateful for them all. Book projects can take years and be touched by so many helping hands, but we are especially appreciative in this last year for the efforts of Hayley Daen, Nikki Moore, Erin Ragoon, Julia Regner, and Erin Simpson, who were dedicated, creative, and hard working, adding so much to our efforts.

Our daily work and organizational tasks for this book were made far easier by the detailed and dedicated Beth Price. Her diligence and dogged determination kept us on task. Her invention and management of our recipe-testing system proved invaluable. All of these recipes work, and we have Beth and her online recipe-tester recruits to thank for it.

Other resources are numerous as well. They include cookbook author Damon Fowler, who came to stay in Charleston one time when we were buried in biscuits and talked to us more about some of his favorites from his own books, as well as things he has learned in his scholarly research over the years. Shirley Corriher and Kate Almand, who are a bit entwined as well, have been my source of information and techniques since the 1970s.

Other friends have given us their recipes over the years, and we have tried to credit them as well.

Mrs. S. R. Dull, whose book *Southern Cooking* I have studied and cooked from for the same forty years, and Irma Rombauer's *Joy of Cooking*, which has been with me even longer, are two of our most important teachers. Their names and books are in the bibliography section along with many others. I have collected many recipes, books, and pamphlets from White Lily flour over the years and have learned from them equally. They were our public television underwriter when Cynthia and I worked together on *New Southern Cooking* and brought us into the world of soft-wheat flour. They became our sponsor because they said I was the first person to put in writing, in an article in *Brown's Guide to Georgia*, what made their flour different. Although management has changed, the flour has not, and we have tested the recipes in this book with it as well as with other flours.

—Nathalie Dupree
December 2010

Foreword by Terry Kay

BISCUITS

My mother baked biscuits three times a day. No one on Earth made them better. Of course, feeding a dozen children and an appreciative and hungry farmer-husband gave her an edge in the practice. After her death, my father eventually resorted to canned biscuits, declaring them only passably eatable, yet I could always hear the unsaid end of the sentence, ". . . but not half as good as your mama could make them."

When writing *To Dance with the White Dog*, I remembered the occasion that my father decided to bake biscuits and how comically tragic the experiment became. It inspired what I have always called the biscuit-cooking scene in the book—my favorite scene from all the stories I've written and the only scene I really enjoy reading aloud.

Following is that scene. I am overjoyed with presenting it again in this extraordinary cookbook celebrating the true soul food of mankind—the biscuit. My mother would have rejoiced in what my friends Nathalie Dupree and Cynthia Graubart have created. Of course, at the mixing bowl she would have kept to her own recipe, and, for me, that is the only thing missing from *Southern Biscuits*. Still, having that recipe wouldn't have mattered. Only my mother could do it the way it ought to be done—her way.

"Kate called before sundown and, minutes later, Carrie called. Both wanted to know if he would have dinner with them. He refused both offers, telling them he was not hungry, but he was, and he decided he would bake fresh biscuits and have biscuits and molasses.

"It would not be hard to bake biscuits, he thought. He had sat at the kitchen table hundreds of times and watched her at the cabinet, her hands flashing over the dough, and it did not seem a hard thing to do. He knew the ingredients she used.

"He stood at the cabinet and took the wood mixing bowl and scooped three cups of flour from the flour bin, and then he measured out two teaspoons of baking powder and a teaspoon of baking soda and a teaspoon of salt and he mixed it together with his hands. Then he took up a palmful of shortening from the can and dropped it into the middle of the flour mixture, but it did not seem enough and he added another palmful and he began to knead the shortening and flour mixture together, but it was greasy and stuck to his hands.

"The dog watched him from the doorway leading into the middle room. 'Don't think I know what I'm doing, do you?' he said to the dog. 'Think I forgot about the buttermilk, don't you?' He had forgotten, and talking to the dog reminded him. He pulled across the room on his walker and took the buttermilk from the refrigerator and returned to the cabinet and began to pour the milk over the wad of dough. 'Ought to be enough,' he judged aloud. 'Can't be that hard to make biscuits.' He kneaded the buttermilk into the shortening-and-flour mixture and the dough became like glue, sticking to his fingers. 'Need some more flour,' he said profoundly to the dog. The dog tilted her head curiously.

"He worked for another thirty minutes with the dough, adding flour and buttermilk and shortening until it caked on his fingers, and then he decided the dough was firm enough and he rolled it out on waxed paper and cut it with the cutter. He had fifty-two biscuits. 'Great God,' he said in amazement. 'I just wanted two or three.'

"The biscuits were not eatable. They were flat and hard and were colored a murky yellow. He put one in front of the dog and the dog sniffed and looked up at him sadly and trotted away. 'Don't know what's good, do you?' he said. He wiped butter across the top of two of the biscuits and poured molasses over them and cut one with his knife and tasted it. He spit the biscuit from his mouth and sat at the table and laughed silently.

"She would be laughing, too, he thought. Or scowling. Thinking him an old fool for trying to do something that she had done with ease. Got to get one of the girls to show me how to cook biscuits, he decided. Can't be that hard."

Terry Kay. *To Dance with the White Dog.* Atlanta: Peachtree Publishers, Ltd., 1990. Used with permission.

Introduction

WHAT IS A BISCUIT?

A biscuit was originally made out of flour and water, the basis of hardtack carried by early travelers. Ultimately, a little lard was added, the dough was beaten hours before shaping and baking, the final product holding a little slivered country ham, becoming a gourmet's delight called a Beaten Biscuit. (We now make it with a food processor in five minutes.)

Once baking powder was developed in the 1800s—replacing the potash that had been used as a leavening—it was added to the same flour and water and, mixed together and shaped into a round, it became a biscuit. (These are still eaten today as Dorm Biscuits.) Any other addition is an extension of the cook's imagination, whether whole milk, buttermilk, sour cream, yogurt, whipping cream, shortening, lard, or butter are used. Each adds a different capacity for leavening or flavoring.

The lightest biscuits are made out of delicate white winter-wheat flour, also called "soft wheat" due to its low gluten content. With the addition of a fat and a liquid, usually milk or buttermilk, they are a close cousin to scones, containing sugar and possibly an egg, which the English fill with clotted cream and raspberries and serve for tea, not for breakfast or another meal. The English biscuit, which is a cookie, bears no relation to a scone. The French have a cake-type called "biscuit," which is

neither cookie, bread, nor scone. There was no agreement over the years about how to spell, define, or pronounce the name of our bread. It just was.

No two cooks make the same biscuit. Some are skinny and thin, crisp all around the outside, baked separated on a pan so they brown all over, and neither wilt nor crumble when covered with pan gravy from ham or sausage. There are thick, plush biscuits, almost too thick to sink one's teeth into. Tender ones butt each other in a round cake pan, so none of the sides are exposed; then they're slathered with butter to keep the exterior soft, and nearly break apart just as they are eaten. Crispy biscuits are rolled thin and separated on the baking sheet, and their buttery, flaky crumbs are snatched up and eaten too. Small biscuit bites hold slivers of ham at cocktail parties, and a popular one now is one to two inches high, sufficiently thick to split in two, and sturdy enough to hold pork tenderloin or chicken breast—great for picnics.

So, the question is: Should a biscuit melt and break up in one's mouth, oozing with butter, or be firm enough to sandwich a piece of sausage or pork tenderloin without crumbling? Only the cook can answer.

My first biscuits were hard little rocks of dough capable of breaking teeth. I had grown up with my mother's. She would pull a box of biscuit mix out of the cabinet, add a little milk or water to some of the contents, and throw

them diffidently in the oven, grateful if they were neither raw nor burned. My goal was to have people lie in bed in the morning, thinking, "If I could just have a hot biscuit like Nathalie's, I'd get out of bed."

Then I learned that biscuit-making takes knowledge and technique because no one is born knowing how to make them, and few still have the joy of watching another—a mother or grandmother once upon a time—making biscuits day after day. But making biscuits is something every Southerner should learn because they are the perfect accompaniment to the Southern meal. (Well, actually, I'm told biscuits are baked all over the United States—for much the same reasons: time and money. Many of them are not as light, for reasons to be explained.) Learning to cook Southern biscuits enables freedom from commercial fast food and frozen biscuits, inferior biscuits to homemade ones. And it satisfies the soul. People using this book will be able to make biscuits that will make their children weep for them when they are dead and gone just to eat their biscuits again.

Many years ago at Rich's Cooking School in Atlanta, my students (including Shirley Corriher) and I embarked on our own search for the perfect biscuit for an article in *Brown's Guide to Georgia* magazine. We tried recipes from cookbooks, sampled the tried-and-true techniques of old friends, and judged the biscuits on a scale of 1 to 10 based on color, fluffiness, moistness, crispness of exteriors,

and taste. Kate Almand's and Shirley Corriher's recipes, different as they are, were as close to perfection as any we found. We are still looking and learning, from Junior League and church cookbooks, food editors and writers, and tomes of "how to" cooking and baking books. (See our bibliography on page 212.) Finally, I should say that to make the finest true-Southern biscuits requires something my colleagues and I call a touch of grace—a blessing some people share—which can be acquired with patience and care.

A SOUTHERN BISCUIT

I never met a biscuit I didn't like. Fat, skinny, crumbly, tender, moist, tall, hard, stuffed, flavored, short, tart, blousy, tiny, sweet, cheesy, or creamy—they all have their own origins and reasons for being, from economic and availability to personal preference and commercial viability.

In the past, a large poor family might have cooked batch after batch, using little fat, keeping them small and hard enough to carry the thick pan gravy left over after frying a small amount of country ham. And those going on a long journey or to war might have carried biscuits hard as coal to soak in coffee made from roasted okra leaves or a chocolate drink made from the troops' generous chocolate ration, chocolate being an untaxed cheap product in the Americas at the time. Or a rich man's cook likely served tender, melt-in-the-mouth, whipped cream biscuits spread with the finest fruit jams made from his abundant garden.

The iconic Southern biscuit is a round (or possibly square), tender, flaky creation of flour and liquid, somewhat similar to a scone, hot out of the oven and ready to split and fill with melting butter, jam or jelly, sausage, or country ham and pepper jelly; or to hollow out a pocket for honey, sorghum, or other molasses, making a receptacle fit for taking to school or the field, or for nibbling a cold snack in the middle of the night.

My ideal Southern biscuit is feathery light with a light brown crust on the top and a moist interior. It may have slight indentations on the sides where it has bumped into other biscuits as it baked. It will split easily and cleanly. It will begin to crumble just as the last bit of sautéed pork loin it holds is eaten, and not before. There are people who want a crispy, nearly hard crust and sides. Other people want biscuits that are small enough to fit in the cup of their hand or sturdy enough to put in a backpack. Well, here they all are! We hope we have a biscuit for everyone!

Making biscuits from scratch is faster than defrosting and baking a store-bought frozen biscuit. Making our refrigerator mix of the flour, baking powder, and fat (lard, shortening, butter, cream cheese, etc.) is an easy way to speed up the process. Just adding liquid to a premeasured amount of homemade mix makes biscuits, waffles, pancakes, coffee cakes, and a panoply of cheese straws and other appetizers. Adding a bit of yeast produces make-ahead dough for Angel Biscuits (page 96) that can be baked any time within a week.

To find the best biscuits, we tested innumerable recipes over a period of years. Some accompany eggs on the morning plate or ham at the dinner table; others are made with butter and beer to accompany a bowl of chili. Using parslied chicken broth as the liquid makes a spectacular topping for a chicken or meat pot pie as does dropping as dumplings into chicken soup.

We found dozens of ways to use leftover baked biscuits, from splitting and frying in bacon grease on a cold morning or toasting and spreading with cinnamon-butter to be relished with a pot of coffee or tea and a good friend. Crumbled baked biscuits can be used for overnight soufflés, stuffing for turkeys, a thickener for tomato casserole, with or without crumbled cornbread in a meat loaf, stuffed squash, and more. These are lighter and more supple by-products than those made with yeast bread. Bread and summer puddings are among the many desserts. Whatever the baker's choice, nothing beats the pleasure of a Southern biscuit.

Biscuit Basics

FLOUR FACTS

Historically, wheat was either "winter wheat" or "spring wheat." Winter wheat was planted in the fall and harvested in the spring and was known as "soft wheat." Spring wheat was planted in the spring and harvested before the frost and was known as "hard" wheat. Bleaching the flour to ensure a snowy white product tenderizes the flour as well, producing a lighter biscuit.

Flour is categorized by its protein content. The higher protein flours, made mostly from hard wheat, are used when developing the gluten for breads. The lower protein flours, made from soft wheat, are used to keep biscuits, cakes, and piecrusts tender and flaky. English wheat is softer than European wheat, and Southern colonists became accustomed to the softer wheat. Now, all sorts of flours are mixed to give specific results, and "Northern" vs. "Southern" flour is not an issue as many varieties can be grown in the region.

Bread flour contains more than 12 grams of protein per cup. The protein helps develop the gluten, which also gives the bread its chewy texture and crisp crust.

National brands of all-purpose flour contain 11 to 12 grams of protein per cup. This flour is suitable for most baked goods but not for the lightest biscuits. The combination of national brand all-purpose flour and baking powder produces a sturdy biscuit. In the South,

we use a soft-wheat flour with baking powder added or a Southern self-rising flour, known for producing a more tender and fluffier biscuit. If using a national brand, remove 2 or so tablespoons of flour to start to be sure the dough does not become too dry.

Certain brands of Southern flours, like White Lily Flour and Martha White, are made exclusively from soft wheat and contain closer to 9 grams of protein per cup.

Cake flour is a specialty flour with 6 to 8 grams of protein per cup. To make cake flour, mix together ¾ cup of all-purpose flour and 2 tablespoons of cornstarch.

The best-for-biscuits flours include Southern Biscuit, White Lily, Martha White, and Red Band. Very good substitutes include mixtures of cake flour and/or all-purpose flour.

Using Self-rising or All-purpose Flours:

Self-rising flour is packaged with baking powder and salt already added. All-purpose flours need these added. I don't have much patience with people who sneer at self-rising flour, as I don't think they make many biscuits themselves. And, my goodness, is it easy to use! I wager most can't tell the difference blindfolded. Some people add more rising products to make an even lighter biscuit, according to personal preference. Buttermilk and other acid products can change the ratio of leaveners as well.

Differences in flour.

If self-rising flour is not available, whisk together 1 cup all-purpose Southern flour (which, like self-rising flour, has lower gluten), 1 teaspoon salt, and 1½ teaspoons baking powder. Better yet, multiply the ingredients to make a big batch to be kept in the refrigerator or freezer and pulled out when needed. If Southern flour is not available, substitute 1 cup of soft wheat flour or mix ½ cup each of all-purpose and cake flour. Whisk in 1 teaspoon salt and 1½ teaspoons baking powder, and a suitable substitute for Southern self-rising flour is produced. We call this method "making homemade self-rising flour."

TO MAKE SELF-RISING FLOUR

Sift together 1 cup all-purpose flour (or ½ cup cake flour with ½ cup all-purpose flour), ½ to 1 teaspoon salt, and 1½ teaspoons baking powder.

Storing flour:

Flour should stay fresh for a few weeks if stored in an airtight container at room temperature. Put the container in the refrigerator to extend the life to 3 months. Stored in the freezer, the flour stays fresh for 12 months. Bring the flour to room temperature before using.

Measuring flour:

Measuring correctly is an art worth cultivating. Purchase a set of dry measuring cups and at least one wet measuring cup, preferably more of each. A dry measuring cup allows the cook to fill the cup to the rim before leveling off the contents with the back of a knife. A wet measuring cup (preferably glass or see-through) has a space above the measuring mark that allows the liquid to come up to the mark—in a dry measuring cup, the liquid would overflow. Using a wet measuring cup will cause dry products, particularly flour, to pack into the cup. Using a dry measuring cup for the liquids will cause them to be skimpy. To see if they are both correctly manufactured, measure a cup of water in the wet measuring cup and pour it into the dry. It should come dangerously close to the brim. Unfortunately, giveaway and cheap measuring cups may be off the mark and have to be discarded.

A cup of Southern flour weighs 4 ounces, but only if measured correctly. When a bag of flour is shipped, the flour settles in the bag. A packed cup of flour can weigh 5 ounces. The best way to achieve an accurate measure is to weigh the flour; but, alas, our lives are not perfect, so the second best way to measure is to use a whisk or long spoon to stir the flour in the bag. Now lightly spoon the flour into the dry measuring cup and level off the top with the back of a knife. When pouring the flour into the mixing bowl, notice if the flour breaks up or stays in the shape of the cup. If it is cup-shaped, remove two or three tablespoons of flour as that is a sign the flour was too tightly packed—it's always easier to add flour to a dough and harder to take away.

BAKING POWDER

The first modern version of baking powder was discovered and manufactured in 1843 by Alfred Bird, a British chemist, so he could make yeast-free bread for his wife, Elizabeth, who had allergies to eggs and yeast. It was further improved and formulated by Eben Horsford, who patented it as Baking Powder, the first calcium phosphate baking powder.

Around 1880, it was discovered that alum and baking soda made a stronger and cheaper leavening but left a distinct unpleasant aftertaste. In 1889, Calumet Baking Powder was marketed as the first double-acting baking powder whose leavening began in the bowl and repeated in the hot oven.

Most commercially available baking powders are made up of an alkaline component, baking soda, acid salts, and cornstarch or potato starch. Baking soda is the source of the carbon dioxide. The corn or potato starch is used to absorb moisture, which prolongs shelf life, flows more easily, and allows the baking powder to be measured more accurately by increasing the bulk.

The acid in a baking powder can be either fast-acting or slow-acting. A fast-acting acid reacts in a wet mixture with baking soda at room temperature. A slow-acting acid will not react until heated in an oven. Baking powders that contain both fast- and slow-acting acids are double acting; those that contain only one acid are single-acting. By providing a second rise in the oven, double-acting baking powders increase the reliability of baked goods by rendering the time elapsed between mixing and baking less critical. Single-acting baking powders need to be baked right away. Use nonaluminum baking powders such as Rumford, Bakewell Cream, and Red Star. Calumet and Clabber Girl contain aluminum.

Baking powder usually should be replaced if much more than six months old as it loses its leavening capacity over time. Make a habit of writing the date of purchase on the container. To test baking powder for freshness, add a cup of hot water to 2 teaspoons of baking powder. It should immediately begin sizzling and foam up. If not, discard the container and replace with a new one.

Using baking soda or baking powder:

Some recipes call for baking soda while others call for baking powder, depending on the other ingredients in the recipe.

Baking powder contains both an acid and a base and has an overall neutral effect in terms of taste when it is free of aluminum. Recipes that call for baking powder often call for other neutral-tasting ingredients, such as milk. Sodium bicarbonate is the source of the leavening power in both baking soda and baking powder.

Baking soda is pure sodium bicarbonate and needs to be mixed with an acidic ingredient—such as chocolate, honey, molasses, citrus juice, sour cream, buttermilk, or brown sugar—to release the carbon dioxide that leavens the dough and prevents a bitter aftertaste. This is why recipes that already contain acidic ingredients may call for baking soda rather than for baking powder. The baking soda neutralizes any acidic ingredients in the recipe, such as yogurt, buttermilk, or sour cream.

Since baking powder already contains the acid component to react with the sodium bicarbonate, it is not necessary to have acidic ingredients in the recipe. One teaspoon of baking powder contains ¼ teaspoon of baking soda, meaning that baking soda is four times more powerful than baking powder.

Adding *both* baking powder and baking soda:

Some recipes will call for both baking soda and baking powder. In this case, baking powder is used for its reliability—guaranteeing the acid matches the amount of soda, and the double-acting process will help give a good rise. The combination of baking powder and additional baking soda may make a busty biscuit, but we find that this creates an aftertaste. One exception, which none of us could taste, was the sour cream butter biscuit from the book *My Mother's Southern Kitchen* by Jim Villa with his mother. Baking powder already contains sufficient acid to activate. Baking soda needs acid to activate. For this reason, some people prefer using baking soda when another acid such as buttermilk or sour cream is added—they are afraid that using baking powder will make it too acidic. I prefer the tang that accompanies baking powder, and I find self-rising flour easiest. If there is a disagreement with this, feel free to switch every recipe to baking soda, remembering to add salt and an acid such as cornstarch, cocoa, buttermilk, sour cream, and the like to activate it.

THE RIGHT FAT

A little fat—whether lard, shortening, butter, cream cheese, or goat butter—tenderizes and moistens as well as adds flavor to biscuits.

Butter tastes best, but lard and shortening make a lighter, flakier, more layered biscuit. The lightest fats are leaf lard, shortening, and goat-milk butter, followed by stick margarine (only used in Buttermilk-Margarine Biscuits, page 94). Butter produces heavier biscuits but gives the most flavor, color, and layering. Some people combine two or even three fats to come up with a product combining lightness, color, flakiness, and flavor.

Lard and shortening were integral in biscuit making before refrigeration was common because they did not melt,

Fats: Butter, Goat Butter, Crisco, Lard, Leaf Lard

separate, or puddle as butter may when left at a hot room temperature. Lighter and softer to the touch, lard and shortening are more easily combined with the flour.

Modern cooks use cold butter cut in small cubes or pieces, quickly mixed in by hand or with the food processor to increase the flakiness. It can produce a fabulous biscuit, so when we say butter is heavier, it can overcome obstacles if handled correctly. My husband says I should tell everyone that Cynthia and I always leave our butter out, covered, at room temperature. Rock-hard butter is not the same spread on a biscuit or on bread. Soft butter is easier to use for sautéing and really only melts on the counter in the dog days of August. Still, we are all grateful for the durability of lard or shortening in the heat.

Recipes will vary from ¼ cup to ¾ cup fat for each 2 cups of flour. Most call for rubbing or cutting in the fat with the combined dry ingredients sufficiently to make a crumb-like mixture with some larger lumps. It is possible, as with piecrusts, to cut in the fat too much and make the fat disappear. Most of our recipes call for the fat to be cut into two different-size pieces, rubbing in the smaller size until the mixture looks like well-crumbled feta cheese, and then rubbing in the larger size pieces until no piece is left larger than a pea. Shaking the bowl occasionally will allow the larger pieces to bounce to the top of the flour, revealing the largest lumps that still need rubbing. Over-rubbing the fat will prevent the absorption as it melts. The larger fat pieces will "sheet," spreading out into the dough. The smaller pieces of fat combined with the flour will melt quicker than the larger pieces. The smaller pieces aid tenderness, the larger ones flakiness and structure.

The method for "rubbing" in the fat is really more of a thumb and finger snapping motion—sheeting the fat more than cutting into tiny particles. Hands are always better than a machine, but it takes practice.

Not everyone rubs the flour with fat; some talented bakers like Kate Almand mush together the milk and fat in the well of flour until it looks like thick lumpy pancake batter and then proceed to pull the flour into the milk and fat.

The less fat, the lighter the biscuit; the more fat, the crisper, which is a bit counterintuitive.

Drippings

Bacon drippings are obtained by frying the bacon and then pouring the remaining hot fat through a strainer or cloth or sturdy paper towel. The fat will solidify when cool, allowing it to be incorporated into the flour. When I grew up, drippings were on every stove top; my grandmother kept hers in an old Crisco can with a piece of layered cloth cut in a circle and tied around the open can. Chilled, it can be used as lard.

THE RIGHT LIQUID

"Sweet" milk originally was the designation used by Southern farm families for milk fresh from the cow.

Buttermilk originally was the butterless liquid remaining after fat had been separated out of cream in order to make butter, and it had a light, sour flavor. Buttermilk was the milk most often drunk on farms and didn't require cash outlay.

Clabber was milk, primarily fresh buttermilk, that was left unrefrigerated and turned sour in the South's heat. Clabber was common, and it was useful for baking, adding acid that aided in leavening, and had a piquant, tart flavor.

Over time, buttermilk was preferred by many over sweet milk, and, like the French crème fraîche, it became a desirable product. The milk's natural bacteria produced acid that soured and curdled, or clabbered; the milk protein was inhibited when the milk was refrigerated, so the desired consistency and flavor could be reproduced consistently for drinking and baking.

True buttermilk is only produced by unpasteurized milk, as the heating process kills the bacteria. Today's buttermilk is cultured, with special lactic acid added to create and enhance a sour, or tart, flavor, but it is nowhere near the same consistency and flavor of true clabber or buttermilk.

There are various "recipes" for turning pasteurized milk into soured milk: Add 1 tablespoon of lemon juice per cup of pasteurized milk and let sit until curdled, making a sour milk that has a bit of a tang and a thick consistency. Or mix 1 part fresh yogurt (which has a live culture) or sour cream with 8 parts slightly heated pasteurized milk (as one would making a mock crème fraîche), stir, lightly cover, and leave at room temperature overnight or up to two days to let it thicken and develop a sour taste; then refrigerate until ready to use. It has a paler taste than true buttermilk and is "bumpier." Adding fresh milk to a jar of clabber will cause it to clabber as well, so re-clabbering isn't necessary.

Liquid activates the leavening and creates steam, which helps the biscuit to rise. Buttermilk, yogurt, sour cream, and other acidic liquids are more desirable than milk as their tartness adds flavor, and the combination of their acid and the leaveners (baking powder and baking soda) give an added boost, resulting in even more fluffiness than usual. Powdered milks of either kind are effective substitutes for the liquid kind. Cream, sour cream, yogurt, and other milk products may be used on their own with or without added fat, both ways producing exquisite biscuits. We found goat milk to be extraordinary. For tender biscuits, the dough should resemble well-crumbled feta cheese before adding the liquid. Pull the flour into the liquid using broad circular motions just until the dough leaves the side of the bowl and rounds up into a ball.

If using 2 percent milk, less will be needed as it is thinner, and the thinner the liquid, the less is needed. Use what is available, but whole milk and buttermilk make a better biscuit.

BISCUIT PREPARATION

Kneading the biscuits:

Kneading is a broad term, technically meaning a method of handling to produce a smooth dough that traps the gases formed by leaveners (primarily yeast) in a network of stretched and expanded gluten strands. It can take up to 30 minutes by hand or less in a machine. The hand process involves folding and stretching the dough vigorously.

But kneading for a biscuit is the opposite. Rather than vigorous kneading, gentle manipulation of the dough is required. Biscuit dough becomes tough when over-manipulated. It gets its rise from trapping the gases of the leavenings (primarily baking soda). Three things activate and toughen flour—liquid, manipulation, and heat.

The fats tenderize the dough as well as sheeting in the dough and making layers, depending on the amount they are worked into the dough. The liquid moistens the dough and activates the baking powder. The lighter the fat and the lower the gluten level of the flour, the lighter the biscuit. The less watery the liquid, the more it tenderizes the dough. So, cream produces a much lighter biscuit than milk, and milk a much lighter biscuit than water. Milks

CYNTHIA'S REAL-LIFE PANTRY

Some days, I do long for cabinets and shelves lined with matching labeled containers and the unending resources of time and money to cook as I please and to wander the aisles of the expensive specialty grocery stores; but that is a short-lived fantasy. While Nathalie enjoys the freedom of a house without children, a rotating staff of interns in the kitchen who both cook and shop, and a husband who does the dishes at night, I am a mom who struggles to keep enough milk in the house for two teenagers and enough toilet paper on hand for a house with five bathrooms.

My baking pantry reflects my circumstances and my personality. I am not a baker. Discovering the biscuits for the Easy Biscuit chapter was my salvation. I'm not likely to have baking powder in my pantry (well, at least not fresh), and the only reason I have baking soda is due to the leftovers from the baking soda–vinegar volcano-science-project phase my children went through.

Self-rising flour came into my life while I was producing Nathalie's television series, *New Southern Cooking*. Our sponsor was White Lily Foods, and Nathalie created the best cobbler recipe using self-rising flour. I went from a non-baker who served store-bought desserts to a cook who had at least one fabulous homemade dessert she could put on the table (Lazy Girl Peach Cobbler, page 200).

Aside from the self-rising flour always in my pantry, I do keep a wide variety of dairy products in the refrigerator. We drink 2 percent milk, so rarely do we have whole milk available. My daughter, the dancer, lives on Greek yogurt, so we always have plenty around, and my husband sees clients at home, so I keep half-and-half in the fridge for when he serves coffee. Those ingredients in various combination create Busty Yogurt Biscuits (page 44) and, of course, Cynthia's Real Life Pantry Biscuits (page 48).

Quite some time ago, I made my peace with butter, although it took my cholesterol-phobic husband much longer to give up his butter substitutes. I now purchase butter on sale and store it in the freezer so we are never without.

As for greasing pans and baking dishes, I once was a devotee of cooking spray. Eventually, all of my bakeware developed stains that I've been unable to remove. I went back to using vegetable oil, butter, or shortening.

with acid—such as clabber, unpasteurized buttermilk, sour cream, or yogurt—boost the strength of the baking soda to lighten the product.

Manipulation develops the gluten just enough to smooth the dough, letting the flour "hold" the fat in suspension and causing sheets of the fat to make a flakier and perhaps layered dough to incorporate the ingredients. The layering is enhanced, not by kneading like bread but by folding. We recommend two kinds of manipulation for biscuits:

1. The first is folding the dough when the dough is to be patted and cut out. We fold the dough in half twice before patting out and cutting out the biscuit dough. Some people fold a dozen times, others fold in thirds, like a letter, many times. We stick with our two-time two-fold method for the novice. However, as a baker develops skill in biscuit baking, more folding may be added to some doughs to increase the flakiness and thus the rise.

2. The second is hand-shaping. Each performs the function of manipulating the dough, allowing a much nicer rise in the dough. Alas, this is not something that can be taught by words, but must come to the baker through experience and touch. We hope each baker gets to this point.

Shaping the dough:

Shaping the dough is the most difficult element for some. Hand rolling and shaping takes practice, just as hitting a golf

Fold the dough in half.

ball does. To achieve really perfect biscuit making, make a number of practice batches and write down the best technique. No one made a perfect biscuit the first time, not even one's mother-in-law. Why spending money on golf is allowed and practicing making biscuits is not is a sad commentary.

There are numerous ways to shape dough. Kate Almand uses some of the self-rising flour left in the biscuit bowl, as do I. Shirley uses plain (not self-rising) flour for shaping because she prefers its "finish." Use what is available.

Methods for shaping

1. Hand-shaping 1: Flour hands, pull a biscuit-sized piece of dough from the mass, dip the exposed (wet) part of the dough in flour, then roll the bottom in one cupped floured palm, simultaneously turning with thumb and pinkie while smoothing the top with the other palm. Give the dough a final pat. It sounds like patting one's head while rubbing one's stomach, but it is doable with practice.

2. Hand-shaping 2: After patting out the dough into a round of the desired height, divide the dough into four pieces. Divide each of those into three more pieces. Roll each section between two palms to make a round. It is okay for it to be rough and bumpy.

3. Cutting: Roll or pat out the dough on a floured board, then cut with a biscuit cutter, being careful not to twist the cutter. For a biscuit that splits open easily, fold the dough in half before cutting through the two layers.

4. Scooping: Shirley Corriher, my student from many years ago at Rich's Cooking School, has gone on to fame for her biscuits and two best-selling books. She now uses a nonstick or floured ice-cream scoop, dipping it into the flour before scooping out the very wet dough—much like a drop biscuit—into a greased cake pan, filling it with rounded biscuits, and, like Kate's, "bumping" each

biscuit in the pan. This technique of putting them in a cake pan allows the biscuits to be held on all sides, from both the pan and each other, enabling the dough to be wetter and keeping them from spreading out, which would make them thinner and crisper.

5. Dropping: Drop biscuits can be a much wetter dough. Use a large floured spoon or ice cream scoop to scoop the unkneaded wet dough and drop the biscuits onto a greased pan, a hot soup, or a casserole as if it were a dumpling (page 154).

6. Folding: Flour a tea towel well. Move the dough to the towel, fold over part of the towel on the dough, and gently pat the towel to flatten the underlying dough. Remove the towel and cut or shape as above. Brush off any excess flour (page 58).

7. Marking: Flip the entire unshaped dough to a 9-inch square pan. Pat down to smooth the top. Mark off squares, cutting halfway down, and bake until brown. Remove from the oven and cut the squares out of the pan.

8. Using a ring or square: Place the ring on a baking sheet and then pat the dough level with the sides of the form. When baked, remove ring or square and cut into equal-sized biscuits.

Scraps of dough

Reworked scraps of dough may not be company-perfect, but there is a special treat for cook and cook's helpers in sprinkling the scraps with cinnamon sugar before baking. Don't bother making into regular shapes—enjoy the strange shapes remaining after cutting the rounds. Scraps should be patted together, not gathered into a ball or kneaded.

Cutting the biscuits:

Cutting biscuits makes new cooks feel more secure. Biscuit cutters are sold individually or in sets, ranging from ½-inch diameter up to 4-inch diameter and have a straight sharp edge. It can be done with anything from empty cans to glasses. Round-edged products such as a glass lack a sharp edge and may squoosh the exterior and prevent the layering around the edges. Beware of twisting the cutter as it presses down on the dough. This too creates an irregular exterior as well as pushing down the sides, which prevents the biscuit from rising.

Mini biscuits

When baking biscuits that are cut smaller than the recipe indicates, be sure to watch the cooking time. Check on the biscuits partway. If they are not browning sufficiently in what seems like the right amount of time, but feel sturdy on the exterior, remove from the oven. Turn the oven to broil and return the biscuits to the oven to broil, leave the door ajar, and watch carefully until just lightly brown. This will keep them moister than baking until brown, as the insides would not remain moist and tender. If they brown too quickly on the bottom, slide another baking sheet underneath for insulation.

THE RIGHT PAN

Whether using a baking sheet, cake pan, pizza pan, oven-proof or iron skillet, use the same pan over and over again to become familiar with it and to "season" it. Avoid scrubbing harshly or washing in the dishwasher as this will reduce or eliminate the seasoned coating. If the pan is washed in the dishwasher, it will need to be greased occasionally. Initially, greasing the pan results in "frying" the bottom of the biscuit but is absolutely necessary if the pan is unseasoned. If tender or less brown biscuit bottoms are desired, layer two baking sheets or two cake pans, top with parchment paper, and add the shaped dough. Baking in an oven-proof or iron skillet gives a crustier bottom. A dark pan tends to burn more quickly than a light one, so bake in iron or dark pans carefully. A round pan is preferred to a traditional cookie sheet for soft-edged biscuits because it allows the biscuits to snuggle closer together. The pan should accommodate the number of biscuits. Oversized or deep-rimmed pans slow the browning of the biscuits because the hot air takes longer to reach the biscuits.

Placing the biscuits:

Placing biscuits close to each other keeps the sides from browning, making the biscuits more tender, and they prop each other up. Separating them on the pan makes a crisper biscuit, with the biscuits spreading and becoming thinner. Using an 8- or 9-inch cake pan, pizza pan or oven-proof skillet keeps them tight enough together that they help each other rise, the sides where they touch sheltered from browning.

THE RIGHT TEMPERATURE

Much depends on the oven. Every oven is different. Newer convection and double ovens can be particularly problematic, especially if the heat seems to come from the bottom, browning the biscuit bottom rather than the top. If the baking sheets are touching the sides of the oven, the air won't circulate and the bottoms will brown. I advise cooks purchasing new ovens to take a batch of biscuit dough to the vendor's showroom and bake them there before they buy an oven. An equally good idea is to test a home oven (page 29). If need be, rotate the pan halfway through the baking time. My personal preference is the same as Kate's: setting the rack one shelf above the middle shelf, but not so close to the top of the oven that the biscuits hit the top as they rise; using a very hot oven (450 to 500 degrees F); and cooking the biscuits quickly. Whatever works for the cook is the best method. Most of the recipes in this book call for 425 or 450 degrees F because it is easier to burn a biscuit at a high heat than it is to cook it too long. Practice makes perfect.

FROZEN BISCUITS

Unbaked shaped biscuits freeze very well. Freeze unbaked prepared biscuits on a baking sheet covered loosely with plastic wrap. When frozen, move the biscuits to resealable plastic bags and keep in the freezer for up to one month.

With yeast products such as Angel Biscuits (page 96), it is best to bake them before freezing as unbaked products may become tough and have poor texture and volume. When freezing yeast products unbaked, add ½ teaspoon more yeast to compensate for any loss of rise from freezing.

Baking Homemade Frozen Biscuits:

Preheat the oven according to the recipe. Move the frozen biscuits to a baking sheet and bake for 5 minutes longer than the recipe directs.

Baking Commercial Frozen Biscuits:

There are always times when frozen foods are justified. Frozen biscuits are no different. Consider, however, that most store-bought biscuits take longer from start to finish, including defrosting the frozen biscuits to room temperature and preheating the oven.

LEFTOVER BISCUITS

Wrap cool biscuits in a resealable plastic bag or aluminum foil and refrigerate. They keep a few days. The sour cream, whipping cream, and goat butter biscuits are almost like new the second day. See our Leftover Biscuits recipe for more instructions (page 99).

Reheating biscuits:

Method 1—Preheat the oven to 400 degrees F. Wrap leftover or baked-ahead biscuits, scones, and muffins in a single layer in aluminum foil and heat until hot, about 10 to 15 minutes.

Method 2—Split and spread the biscuits with butter and toast them in the broiler until they're hot and lightly browned; or, before toasting, spread them with shredded cheese, cream cheese, pimento cheese, jelly, poppy seeds, or sesame seeds.

COMMON ISSUES WITH BISCUITS

Working with the dough:

Too floury or dry

Flour is different every day. It changes due to the weather, whether absorbing or losing moisture from the air. If measuring rather than weighing (as exacting pastry chefs do), there will be variations in the amount of flour used. Additionally, some buttermilks, creams, yogurts, etc., are thicker than others. A pastry brush or clean small paintbrush is helpful to brush off any extra flour on the exterior before the biscuits go into the oven. A little extra liquid will take up any excess flour still in the bowl. Rather than roll out an already dry dough, try hand-shaping, which uses less flour (see the directions on pages 24–25).

Too wet

Wetness in a dough can be deceiving. In the bowl, it may seem gloppier than it should be, but remember that it is better to have a wet dough than a dry one; flour can always be added. Folding it helps determine if more flour is needed than the ¼ cup of reserved flour called for in the recipe. A slightly wet dough, whose additional steam pushes it up and out, will be more tender than a dry dough when baked.

Working with the oven:

First, get an oven thermometer and check the accuracy of the thermostat. Many thermostats are easy for the cook to adjust. If not, check with the manufacturer to see how to get it done. If your oven regularly runs at a different temperature than that on the thermometer, adjust the temperature accordingly. To see how evenly an oven bakes, spread a large baking sheet (at least one inch smaller all around than the oven so the air can circulate) with pieces of white loaf bread nestled next to each other. Bake in a preheated 350 degree oven for 5 to 10 minutes. After removing, take a look at the areas that are uneven and plan accordingly, either rotating any baked items or avoiding a section of the oven altogether. Check the underneath side of the bread to note differences in color between top and bottom, side to side. If the underneath side of the biscuits is over-browning, get a heavier pan or slide a second pan underneath.

Where to bake the biscuits in the oven is debatable. Kate has always cooked her smaller biscuits quick and high—500 degrees F on the top shelf for 7 to 8 minutes. Larger biscuits need a lower temperature—about 425 degrees F—and a middle rack. That said, the bottoms may brown too quickly on the middle rack, so move the biscuits to the top rack to finish. Run under the broiler if they are close to being done and still not lightly dappled with brown.

Uneven or no browning

As heating elements have moved from the top to the bottom of the ovens, it has become harder to brown in some ovens. Try different shelves of the oven, including putting the racks at the very top and bottom to see if browning occurs, as well as testing the oven to see how it browns toast. Check with an oven thermometer. To brown, run the biscuits under the broiler for a few minutes, keeping the oven door open to watch carefully. Sometimes the heat seals the outside of the biscuit, preventing it from rising but not browning or browning too rapidly. Move the biscuits to a lower rack or lower the temperature 25 degrees F.

1. *Whisk the flour.*

2. *Make a hollow or well.*

5. *Add liquid to the flour.*

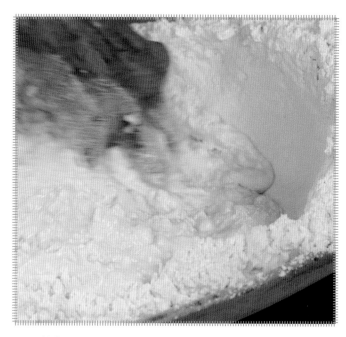
6. *Pull flour into the liquid.*

3. Add the fats.

4. Snap the dough.

7. Incorporate remaining flour into shaggy wettish dough.

8. Get dough ready to turn out.

Easy Biscuits

These recipes are among the easiest of the Southern biscuit repertoire, miraculously requiring only the mixing of any two of a number of ingredients and two steps before baking. They produce biscuits that are simple, hassle-free, painless, uncomplicated, straightforward, effortless, and undemanding. They are the biscuits for the home cook who wants to have fresh biscuits, morning after morning, and is happy to keep plain yogurt in the refrigerator.

The desire to produce the perfect biscuit usually leads the fearful to no biscuits at all. Fearing failure, some cooks quit before they ever start. These biscuits are easy for everyone with just two simple ingredients. This method builds confidence in the baker to produce a light, fluffy biscuit.

The majority of novice biscuit-makers prefer using Southern self-rising flour, readily available in the South, because it eliminates one step in the process—measuring and mixing the baking powder or other leaveners with the flour. Self-rising flour can be kept on the shelf as well as in the refrigerator or freezer. If self-rising is not available in your geographic region, make your own using our recipe (page 17).

These biscuits are all feathery, light, melt-in-the-mouth gems. The Traditional Biscuits in the next chapter are a bit flakier and perhaps hold together better for sandwiching a slice of pork tenderloin or ham to purists, but novices won't miss that at all. Give them a try . . . and bask in the compliments.

Julia Regner's Sturdy Dorm Biscuits

Makes 9 (2-inch) square biscuits

With the likelihood of most families having a homemade refrigerated biscuit mix (see ours on page 50) or commercial biscuit mix in their pantry, this is a very simple and kid-friendly biscuit dish. When Julia was a child, now a college and culinary school graduate, she loved helping her mom in the kitchen. With this recipe, she could escape any potential defeats. As she got older, she found these biscuits very handy to make in the dorm, and they are fancy enough to serve to friends. Sliced in half easily, they are sturdy enough to transform into a ham biscuit sandwich.

2¼ cups Homemade Refrigerator Biscuit Mix (page 50) or commercial biscuit mix, divided

1 cup lukewarm water, divided

Softened butter, for brushing

Preheat oven to 400 degrees F.

For thicker biscuits, butter a 9 x 9-inch square baking pan. For thinner biscuits, butter a 9 x 13-inch baking dish.

Fork-sift or whisk 2 cups of the biscuit mix in a large bowl, preferably wider than it is deep, and set aside the remaining ¼ cup.

Make a deep hollow in the center of the flour with the back of your hand. Pour ⅔ cup of the water into the hollow, reserving ⅓ cup of liquid, and stir with a rubber spatula or large metal spoon, using broad circular strokes to quickly pull the flour into the water. Mix just until the dry ingredients are moistened and the sticky dough begins to pull away from the sides of the bowl. If there is some flour remaining on the bottom and sides of the bowl, stir in 1 to 4 tablespoons of water, just enough to incorporate the remaining flour into the shaggy wettish dough. If the dough is too wet, add a little reserved biscuit mix.

34

Scoop the dough into the prepared baking dish and smooth out the top with a fork. Bake on the top rack of the oven for 13 to 15 minutes, until tinged with brown on top. Remove from the oven and lightly brush the tops with softened or melted butter. Serve from the baking dish by cutting into squares or any desired size.

TIP: Rake the top of the dough with a fork, creating peaks for a crisper top.

TYPES OF LIQUID

Amazingly, fluffy biscuits can be made with just about any liquid. Lightness and rise in a biscuit comes from the liquid and the heat combining to activate the baking powder. Water provides a crisper, sturdier biscuit, whereas whipping cream and sour cream, which also include a bit of fat, produce more tender biscuits.

Allison's Easy Sour Cream Biscuits

Makes 12 to 14 (2½-inch) biscuits

Sour cream biscuits are among the easiest of all the biscuits to make. Using a homemade or commercial self-rising flour makes it easier again, as then only two ingredients are needed. The acid in the milk products tenderizes the biscuits as well as activates the baking powder already incorporated in the flour. This recipe is enormously easy and makes exceedingly tender, moist, and fluffy biscuits with a tang. They have a great rise, to about three times their height.

2¼ cups commercial or homemade self-rising flour (page 17), divided

1¼ cups sour cream, divided

Softened butter, for brushing

Preheat oven to 450 degrees F.

Select the baking pan by determining if a soft or crisp exterior is desired. For a soft exterior, use an 8- or 9-inch cake pan, pizza pan, or oven-proof skillet where the biscuits will nestle together snugly, creating the soft exterior while baking. For a crisp exterior, select a baking sheet or other baking pan where the biscuits can be placed wider apart, allowing air to circulate and creating a crisper exterior, and brush the pan with butter.

Fork-sift or whisk 2 cups of the flour in a large bowl, preferably wider than it is deep, and set aside the remaining ¼ cup.

Make a deep hollow in the center of the flour with the back of your hand. Pour 1 cup of sour cream into the hollow, reserving the remaining ¼ cup, and stir with a rubber spatula or large metal spoon, using broad circular strokes to quickly pull the flour into the sour cream. Mix just until the dry ingredients are moistened and the sticky dough begins to pull away from the sides of the bowl. Use the reserved sour cream as needed to incorporate the remaining flour into the shaggy wettish dough. If the dough is too wet, use more flour when shaping.

Lightly sprinkle a board or other clean surface using some of the reserved flour. Turn the dough out onto the board and sprinkle the top of the dough lightly with flour. With floured hands, fold the dough in half, and pat dough out into a ⅓- to ½-inch-thick round, using a little additional flour only if needed. Flour again if necessary, and fold the dough in half a second time. If the dough is still clumpy, pat and fold a third time. Pat dough out into a ½-inch-thick round for a normal biscuit, ¾-inch-thick for a tall biscuit, and 1-inch-thick for a giant biscuit. Brush off any visible flour from the top. For each biscuit, dip a 2½-inch biscuit cutter into the reserved flour and cut out the biscuits, starting at the outside edge and cutting very close together, being careful not to twist the cutter. The scraps may be combined to make additional biscuits, although these scraps make tougher biscuits. For hand-shaping and other variations, see pages 24–26.

Using a metal spatula if necessary, move the biscuits to the pan or baking sheet. Bake the biscuits on the top rack of the oven for a total of 8 to 10 minutes until light golden brown. After 4 minutes, rotate the pan in the oven so that the front of the pan is now turned to the back, and check to see if the bottoms are browning too quickly. If so, slide another baking pan underneath to add insulation and retard browning. Continue baking another 4 to 6 minutes until the biscuits are light golden brown. When the biscuits are done, remove from the oven and lightly brush the tops with softened or melted butter. Turn the biscuits out upside down on a plate to cool slightly. Serve hot, right side up.

TIP: If the sour cream is too thick, add a little milk. Normally, however, adding milk to thin is not necessary.

Julia's Double Ginger Biscuits

Makes 12 to 14 (2-inch) biscuits

Enjoy these ginger-spiced biscuits of Julia Regner's as an alternative to the family's morning routine. The flavor of ginger adds warmth to the biscuits without making them a too-sweet treat. Try to experiment with other favorite flavors as well. We used one of the newer, stronger ginger ales sold commercially, but any will do.

2¼ cups commercial or homemade self-rising flour (page 17), divided

½ teaspoon ground ginger

¾ cup ginger ale, divided

Softened butter, for brushing

Preheat oven to 400 degrees F.

Select the baking pan by determining if a soft or crisp exterior is desired. For a soft exterior, select an 8- or 9-inch cake pan, pizza pan, or oven-proof skillet where the biscuits will nestle together snugly, creating the soft exterior while baking. For a crisp exterior, select a baking sheet or other baking pan where the biscuits can be placed wider apart, allowing air to circulate and creating a crisper exterior, and brush the pan with butter.

Fork-sift or whisk 2 cups of flour and the ground ginger in a large bowl, preferably wider than it is deep, and set aside the remaining ¼ cup of flour.

Make a deep hollow in the center of the flour with the back of your hand. Slowly pour ½ cup of ginger ale into the hollow, reserving ¼ cup, and stir with a rubber spatula or large metal spoon, using broad circular strokes to quickly pull the flour into the liquid. Mix just until the dry ingredients are moistened and the sticky dough begins to pull away from the sides of the bowl. If there is some flour remaining on the bottom and sides of the bowl, stir in 1 to 4 tablespoons of reserved ginger ale, just enough to incorporate the remaining flour into the shaggy wettish dough. If the dough is too wet, use more flour when shaping.

Lightly sprinkle a board or other clean surface using some of the reserved flour. Turn the dough out onto the board and sprinkle the top of the dough lightly with flour. With floured hands, fold the dough in half, and pat dough out into a ⅓- to ½-inch-thick round, using a little additional flour only if needed. Flour again if necessary and fold the dough in half a second time. If the dough is still clumpy, pat and fold a third time. Pat dough out into a ½-inch-thick round for a normal biscuit, ¾-inch-thick for a tall biscuit, and 1-inch-thick for a giant biscuit. Brush off any visible flour from the top. For each biscuit, dip a 2-inch biscuit cutter into the reserved flour and cut out the biscuits, starting at the outside edge and cutting very close together, being careful not to twist the cutter. The scraps may be combined to make additional biscuits, although these scraps make tougher biscuits. For hand-shaping and other variations, see pages 24–26.

Using a metal spatula if necessary, move the biscuits to the pan or baking sheet. Bake the biscuits on the top rack of the oven for a total of 10 to 14 minutes until light golden brown. After 6 minutes, rotate the pan in the oven so that the front of the pan is now turned to the back, and check to see if the bottoms are browning too quickly. If so, slide another baking pan underneath to add insulation and retard browning. Continue baking another 4 to 8 minutes until the biscuits are light golden brown. When the biscuits are done, remove from the oven and lightly brush the tops with softened or melted butter. Turn the biscuits out upside down on a plate to cool slightly. Serve hot, right side up.

Jennet Alterman's Mother's Shot Glass Biscuits

Makes 30 (½-inch) biscuits

Jennet Alterman, a good friend and an extraordinarily interesting woman, was thrilled to share her mother's recipe for Shot Glass Biscuits. The recipe is easily memorized, and Jennet makes it frequently for these tiny biscuits. The waxed paper method of folding the dough keeps both counters and fingers clean.

2¼ cups Homemade Refrigerator Biscuit Mix (page 50), or commercial biscuit mix, divided

¾ cup milk, divided

¼ cup melted butter

Preheat oven to 400 degrees F.

Select the baking pan by determining if a soft or crisp exterior is desired. For a soft exterior, select an 8- or 9-inch cake pan, pizza pan, or oven-proof skillet where the biscuits will nestle together snugly, helping each other stay tender but rise while baking For a crisp overall exterior, select a baking sheet or other baking pan where the biscuits can be placed wider apart, allowing air to circulate and creating a crisper exterior, and brush the pan with butter.

Fork-sift or whisk 2 cups of the biscuit mix in a large bowl, preferably wider than it is deep, and set aside the remaining ¼ cup.

Make a deep hollow in the center of the flour with the back of your hand. Pour ½ cup of milk, reserving the remaining ¼ cup, and the melted butter into the hollow and stir with a rubber spatula or large metal spoon, using broad circular strokes to quickly pull the flour into the liquids. Mix just until the dry ingredients are moistened and the sticky dough begins to pull away from the sides of the bowl. If there is some flour remaining on the bottom and sides of the bowl, stir in 1 to 4 tablespoons of reserved milk, just enough to incorporate the remaining flour into the shaggy wettish dough If the dough is too wet, add a little of the reserved biscuit mix.

Turn the dough out onto waxed paper. Fold the sheet of waxed paper over the dough and fold the dough in half. Pat dough out into a ⅓- to ½-inch-thick round and fold again in the waxed paper. Pat dough out into a ½-inch round. Working from the outside edge in, dip a shot glass into the reserved mix frequently and cut out the biscuits without twisting. The scraps may be combined to make additional biscuits, although these scraps make tougher biscuits. For hand-shaping and other variations, see pages 24–26.

Using a metal spatula if necessary, move the biscuits to the pan or baking sheet. Bake the biscuits on the top rack of the oven for a total of 10 minutes until light golden brown. After 5 minutes, rotate the pan in the oven so that the front of the pan is now turned to the back, and check to see if the bottoms are browning too quickly. If so, slide another baking pan underneath to add insulation and retard browning. Continue baking another 5 minutes until the biscuits are light golden brown. When the biscuits are done, remove from the oven and lightly brush the tops with softened or melted butter. Turn the biscuits out upside down on a plate to cool slightly. Serve hot, right side up.

Rachel's Very Beginner's Cream Biscuits

Makes 12 to 16 (2½-inch) biscuits

This is a very old recipe found in many books, including the 1964 edition of Joy of Cooking. *It is a snap to make, uncomplicated with few ingredients, yet producing a stunningly tender and fluffy biscuit. There are two Rachels in our lives— my husband's granddaughter, Rachel Bass, and co-author Cynthia's daughter, Rachel Graubart. Novices, we asked them to test recipes we hope will be easy for anyone. Both gave these flying colors for both ease and taste.*

Here's what Gena Berry said about her similar adaptation of this recipe:

A respectable homemade biscuit is an essential part of the Southern table, and this scandalously simple recipe makes turning out the perfect biscuit a snap. This recipe breaks all the rules of southern biscuit-making; there's no shortening to cut in, and you don't even roll out the dough. The results are remarkable and even a novice can turn out fluffy, perfect biscuits in minutes.

Would a respectable Southern lady bend the rules, defy convention and use sneaky shortcuts all in the name of turning out a hot, homemade biscuit? You better believe it!

2¼ cups commercial or homemade self-rising flour (page 17), divided

1¼ cups heavy cream, divided

Preheat oven to 450 degrees F.

Select the baking pan by determining if a soft or crisp exterior is desired. For a soft exterior, select an 8- or 9-inch cake pan, pizza pan, or oven-proof skillet where the biscuits will nestle together snugly, helping each other stay tender but rise while baking. For a crisp overall exterior, select a baking sheet or other baking pan where the biscuits can be placed wider apart, allowing air to circulate and creating a crisper exterior, and brush the pan with butter.

Fork-sift or whisk 2 cups of the flour in a large bowl, preferably wider than it is deep, and set aside the remaining ¼ cup.

Make a deep hollow in the center of the flour with the back of your hand. Pour 1 cup of cream into the hollow, reserving ¼ cup of cream, and stir with a rubber spatula or large metal spoon, using broad circular strokes to quickly pull the flour into the cream. Mix just until the dry ingredients are moistened and the sticky dough begins to pull away from the sides of the bowl. If there is some flour remaining on the bottom and sides of the bowl, stir in 1 to 4 tablespoons of reserved cream, just enough to incorporate the remaining flour into the shaggy wettish dough. If the dough is too wet, use more flour when shaping.

Lightly sprinkle a board or other clean surface using some of the reserved flour. Turn the dough out onto the board and sprinkle the top of the dough lightly with flour. With floured hands, fold the dough in half, and pat dough out into

42

a ⅓- to ½-inch-thick round using a little additional flour only if needed. Flour again if necessary and fold the dough in half a second time. If the dough is still clumpy, pat and fold a third time. Pat dough out into a ½-inch-thick round for a normal biscuit, ¾-inch-thick for a tall biscuit, and 1-inch-thick for a giant biscuit. Brush off any visible flour from the top. For each biscuit, dip a 2½-inch biscuit cutter into the reserved flour and cut out the biscuits, starting at the outside edge and cutting very close together, being careful not to twist the cutter. The scraps may be combined to make additional biscuits, although these scraps make tougher biscuits. For hand-shaping and other variations, see pages 24–26.

Using a metal spatula if necessary, move the biscuits to the pan or baking sheet. Bake the biscuits on the top rack of the oven for a total of 10 to 14 minutes until light golden brown. After 6 minutes, rotate the pan in the oven so that the front of the pan is now turned to the back, and check to see if the bottoms are browning too quickly. If so, slide another baking pan underneath to add insulation and retard browning. Continue baking another 4 to 8 minutes until the biscuits are light golden brown. When the biscuits are done, remove from the oven and lightly brush the top of the biscuits with softened or melted butter. Turn the biscuits out upside down on a plate to cool slightly. Serve hot, right side up.

VARIATION: Cut dough into ½- to 1-inch rounds and bake as directed, adjusting the baking time as necessary. Top with Hot Pepper Jelly (page 176) and serve for cocktails, or split and fill with ham shavings.

VARIATION: HARRIET RIGNY'S EASTER STRAWBERRY SHORTCAKE

My neighbor Harriet Rigny's grandmother made these every Easter for her family. Add a tablespoon or two of sugar to the dough. Line a cake pan with parchment paper. Rather than cut or roll the dough, pat the dough into the lined cake pan. Bake as above, perhaps a few minutes more if necessary to cook through. Remove from the oven, brush the top with softened or melted butter, and turn upside down on a rack to cool slightly. When cool, slice in half horizontally. Sandwich with sugared strawberries and cream, and serve a bowl of each separately.

The 1832 edition of *The Carolina Receipt Book* by a Lady of Charleston (which predates *The Carolina Housewife*) has a recipe for a biscuit that does not get beaten and uses cream and potash, saying it is much better than a beaten biscuit. It is the same size, however, but more like a cream biscuit.

Busty Yogurt Biscuits

Makes 12 (2-inch) biscuits

Yogurt makes a very light, tangy biscuit. With homemade or commercial self-rising flour, it is a simple matter. Yogurt varies in consistency, from the thick cream-topped to the thinner generic brands, so it is always a judgment call as to how much to use to make a wet dough. Do not be tempted to use nonfat or light yogurt as they have additives that will change the nature of the biscuit. But if the yogurt is so thick you can't incorporate it, feel free to add a bit of milk or buttermilk. These crisp biscuits triple in size and cut easily.

2¼ cups commercial or homemade
self-rising flour (page 17), divided

1 teaspoon salt

1 cup plain yogurt, divided

Softened butter, for brushing

Preheat oven to 450 degrees F.

Select the baking pan by determining if a soft or crisp exterior is desired. For a soft exterior, select an 8- or 9-inch cake pan, pizza pan, or oven-proof skillet where the biscuits will nestle together snugly, creating the soft exterior while baking. For a crisp exterior, select a baking sheet or other baking pan where the biscuits can be placed wider apart, allowing air to circulate and creating a crisper exterior, and brush the pan with butter.

Fork-sift or whisk 2 cups of flour and the salt in a large bowl, preferably wider than it is deep, and set aside the remaining ¼ cup of flour.

Make a deep hollow in the center of the flour with the back of your hand. Pour ⅔ cup of yogurt into the hollow, reserving the ⅓ cup yogurt, and stir with a rubber spatula or large metal spoon, using broad circular strokes to quickly pull the flour into the yogurt. Mix just until the dry ingredients are moistened and the sticky dough begins to pull away from the sides of the bowl. If there is some flour remaining on the bottom and sides of the bowl, stir in 1 to 4 tablespoons of reserved yogurt, just enough to incorporate the remaining flour into the shaggy wettish dough If the dough is too wet, use more flour when shaping.

Lightly sprinkle a board or other clean surface using some of the reserved flour. Turn the dough out onto the board and sprinkle the top of the dough lightly with flour. With floured hands, fold the dough in half, and pat dough out into a ⅓- to

½-inch-thick round, using a little additional flour only if needed. Flour again if necessary and fold the dough in half a second time. If the dough is still clumpy, pat and fold a third time. Pat dough out into a ½-inch-thick round for a normal biscuit, ¾-inch-thick for a tall biscuit, and 1-inch-thick for a giant biscuit. Brush off any visible flour from the top. For each biscuit, dip a 2-inch biscuit cutter into the reserved flour and cut out the biscuits, starting at the outside edge and cutting very close together, being careful not to twist the cutter. The scraps may be combined to make additional biscuits, although these scraps make tougher biscuits. For hand-shaping and other variations, see pages 24–26.

Using a metal spatula if necessary, move the biscuits to the pan or baking sheet. Bake the biscuits on the top rack of the oven for a total of 10 to 14 minutes until light golden brown. After 6 minutes, rotate the pan in the oven so that the front of the pan is now turned to the back, and check to see if the bottoms are browning too quickly. If so, slide another baking pan underneath to add insulation and retard browning. Continue baking another 4 to 8 minutes until the biscuits are light golden brown. When the biscuits are done, remove from the oven and lightly brush the tops with softened or melted butter. Turn the biscuits out upside down on a plate to cool slightly. Serve hot, right side up.

Yogurt and Heavy Cream Biscuits

Makes 12 to 14 (2-inch) biscuits

We liked both the yogurt and the heavy cream biscuits, but we wanted a subtler tang for some occasions. Mixing the two ingredients made what those who love buttermilk biscuits crave—a tangy light biscuit!

2¼ cups commercial or homemade self-rising flour (page 17), divided

¾ cup heavy cream, divided

½ cup yogurt

Softened butter, for brushing

Preheat oven to 400 degrees F.

Select the baking pan by determining if a soft or crisp exterior is desired. For a soft exterior, select an 8- or 9-inch cake pan, pizza pan, or oven-proof skillet where the biscuits will nestle together snugly, creating the soft exterior while baking. For a crisp exterior, select a baking sheet or other baking pan where the biscuits can be placed wider apart, allowing air to circulate and creating a crisper exterior, and brush the pan with butter.

Fork-sift or whisk 2 cups of flour in a large bowl, preferably wider than it is deep, and set aside the remaining ¼ cup flour.

Make a deep hollow in the center of the flour with the back of your hand. Pour ½ cup of the heavy cream, reserving ¼ cup, and the yogurt into the hollow and stir with a rubber spatula or large metal spoon, using broad circular strokes to quickly pull the flour into the liquids. Mix just until the dry ingredients are moistened and the sticky dough begins to pull away from the sides of the bowl. If there is some flour remaining on the bottom and sides of the bowl, stir in 1 to 4 tablespoons of the reserved cream, just enough to incorporate the remaining flour into the shaggy wettish dough. If the dough is too wet, use more flour when shaping.

Lightly sprinkle a board or other clean surface using some of the reserved flour. Turn the dough out onto the board and sprinkle the top of the dough lightly with flour. With floured hands, fold the dough in half, and pat dough out into a ⅓- to ½-inch-thick round, using a little additional flour only if

46

needed. Flour again if necessary and fold the dough in half a second time. If the dough is still clumpy, pat and fold a third time. Pat dough out into a ½-inch-thick round for a normal biscuit, ¾-inch-thick for a tall biscuit, and 1-inch-thick for a giant biscuit. Brush off any visible flour from the top. For each biscuit, dip a 2-inch biscuit cutter into the reserved flour and cut out the biscuits, starting at the outside edge and cutting very close together, being careful not to twist the cutter. The scraps may be combined to make additional biscuits, although these scraps make tougher biscuits. For hand-shaping and other variations, see pages 24–26.

Using a metal spatula if necessary, move the biscuits to the pan or baking sheet. Bake the biscuits on the top rack of the oven for a total of 10 to 14 minutes until light golden brown. After 6 minutes, rotate the pan in the oven so that the front of the pan is now turned to the back, and check to see if the bottoms are browning too quickly. If so, slide another baking pan underneath to add insulation and retard browning. Continue baking another 4 to 8 minutes until the biscuits are light golden brown. When the biscuits are done, remove from the oven and lightly brush the tops with softened or melted butter. Turn the biscuits out upside down on a plate to cool slightly. Serve hot, right side up.

Cut biscuits from the outside in.

Cynthia's Real Life Pantry Biscuits

Makes 12 to 14 (2-inch) biscuits

Cynthia lives a largely busy and less than perfect life, and her pantry may lack in depth what most bakers regularly keep on hand. However, she almost always has yogurt and half-and-half in the fridge and self-rising flour in the cupboard. And voila! a spectacular biscuit.

2¼ cups commercial or homemade self-rising flour (page 17), divided

¾ cup half-and-half, divided

½ cup yogurt

Softened butter, for brushing

Preheat oven to 400 degrees F.

Select the baking pan by determining if a soft or crisp exterior is desired. For a soft exterior, select an 8- or 9-inch cake pan, pizza pan, or oven-proof skillet where the biscuits will nestle together snugly, creating the soft exterior while baking. For a crisp exterior, select a baking sheet or other baking pan where the biscuits can be placed wider apart, allowing air to circulate and creating a crisper exterior, and brush the pan with butter.

Fork-sift or whisk 2 cups of the flour in a large bowl, preferably wider than it is deep, and set aside the remaining ¼ cup of flour.

Make a deep hollow in the center of the flour with the back of your hand. Pour ½ cup of the half-and-half, reserving ¼ cup, and the yogurt into the hollow and stir with a rubber spatula or large metal spoon, using broad circular strokes to quickly pull the flour into the liquids. Mix just until the dry ingredients are moistened and the sticky dough begins to pull away from the sides of the bowl. If there is some flour remaining on the bottom and sides of the bowl, stir in 1 to 4 tablespoons of the reserved half-and-half, just enough to incorporate the remaining flour into the shaggy wettish dough. If the dough is too wet, use more flour when shaping.

Lightly sprinkle a board or other clean surface using some of the reserved flour. Turn the dough out onto the board and sprinkle the top of the dough lightly with flour. With floured hands, fold the dough in half, and pat dough out into a ⅓- to

½-inch-thick round, using a little additional flour only if needed. Flour again if necessary and fold the dough in half a second time. If the dough is still clumpy, pat and fold a third time. Pat dough out into a ½-inch-thick round for a normal biscuit, ¾-inch-thick for a tall biscuit, and 1-inch-thick for a giant biscuit. Brush off any visible flour from the top. For each biscuit, dip a 2-inch biscuit cutter into the reserved flour and cut out the biscuits, starting at the outside edge and cutting very close together, being careful not to twist the cutter. The scraps may be combined to make additional biscuits, although these scraps make tougher biscuits. For hand-shaping and other variations, see pages 24–26.

Use a knife to level the flour.

Using a metal spatula if necessary, move the biscuits to the pan or baking sheet. Bake the biscuits on the top rack of the oven for a total of 10 to 14 minutes until light golden brown. After 6 minutes, rotate the pan in the oven so that the front of the pan is now turned to the back, and check to see if the bottoms are browning too quickly. If so, slide another baking pan underneath to add insulation and retard browning. Continue baking another 4 to 8 minutes until the biscuits are light golden brown. When the biscuits are done, remove from the oven and lightly brush the tops with softened or melted butter. Turn the biscuits out upside down on a plate to cool slightly. Serve hot, right side up.

Homemade Refrigerator Biscuit Mix

Makes 10 cups

If making several batches of biscuits a month, or one biscuit at a time, make a flour-and-fat base mixture to add the milk to at a later time. It will keep several months in a tightly covered container in the refrigerator. Combine one part milk or buttermilk with two parts mix for any quantity of biscuits from 4 to 40! Once again, more salt and baking powder are added. This dough can also be used in making coffee cakes, pancakes, waffles, and the like.

10 cups self-rising flour

3 teaspoons salt

5 teaspoons cream of tartar

4 teaspoons baking powder

2 cups chilled shortening, lard, or butter, roughly cut into ½-inch pieces

Fork-sift or whisk the flour, salt, cream of tartar, and baking powder in a very large bowl. Scatter the shortening over the flour and work in by rubbing fingers with the shortening and flour as if snapping thumb and fingers together (or use two forks or knives, or a pastry cutter) until the mixture looks like well-crumbled feta cheese, with no piece larger than a pea. Shake the bowl occasionally to allow the larger pieces of fat to bounce to the top of the flour, revealing the largest lumps that still need rubbing.

Store the mix in the refrigerator in an airtight container until ready to use.

Cut the fat into the dry flour mixture.

Add liquid to dry flour mixture.

Some people prefer a biscuit mix kept in the refrigerator and pulled out at any time for a quick biscuit. Self-rising flour or biscuit mix requires only the quick addition of a simple ingredient to activate the baking soda—ranging from water to heavy cream, sour cream, and yogurt. A few pats after stirring, then cutting, and the biscuits are ready to go in the oven. Some of these can even be made in advance, ready to pop in the oven as guests are chatting over appetizers or as the family gathers at the table.

Traditional Biscuits

Traditional biscuits encompass a number of types of biscuits, from the Beaten Biscuits of the Old South and England (page 84) to Angel Biscuits (page 96), a yeast biscuit sturdy enough to split and fill but light enough to woo. In between are layered, fluffy, feathery, downy, silky, soft, and velvety Southern biscuits.

Unlike the biscuits in the last chapter, these biscuits incorporate an added fat to the liquid and flour mixture. They take a step more technique, from cutting in the fat, to beating with a rolling pin, to using a food processor, easily mastered with a bit of practice. There are a variety of shaping methods here—using a cloth towel, hand-rolling, ice cream–scooping, dropping, rolling and cutting, and even more. The recipes have any of several fats, each one with a different flavor and quality it brings to the biscuit.

Personal preference dictates the choice—or perhaps it is more the biscuit that one was brought up with. Kate's Biscuits (page 62) will catapult the traditional Southerners back into their grandmothers' kitchen, where she used a big wooden bowl and magic hands to pull biscuits out of the bowl and shape them by hand for baking. Others will remember pulling the Baking Powder Biscuits (page 54) out of the oven as a child, perfect for early breakfast, and tucking them into a coat pocket for the walk to school. Those who learned to love biscuits at their favorite fast-food restaurant will be thrilled with Fast-Food Biscuits (page 78). Those who love a little flake in their biscuit will adore Biscuits Supreme (page 66). There is something here for every biscuit lover.

Baking Powder Biscuits

Makes 12 to 18 (2-inch) biscuits

This is the standard biscuit of most regions in the country. The difference here is that Southern all-purpose flour has less gluten. If using a national brand, start with just 1¾ cup of flour, or make a mix of half cake flour and half national-brand all-purpose flour. It has more fat than a humble biscuit, providing more flakiness and flavor. If a more crumbly biscuit is desired, increase the shortening to ¾ cup.

2¼ cups all-purpose flour, divided

1 tablespoon baking powder

1 teaspoon salt

¼ cup chilled shortening, lard, and/or butter, roughly cut into ¼-inch pieces
AND
¼ cup chilled shortening, lard, and/or butter, roughly cut into ½-inch pieces

1 cup milk or buttermilk, divided

Softened butter, for brushing

Preheat oven to 425 degrees F.

Select the baking pan by determining if a soft or crisp exterior is desired. For a soft exterior, use an 8- or 9-inch cake pan, pizza pan, or ovenproof skillet where the biscuits will nestle together snugly, creating the soft exterior while baking. For a crisp exterior, select a baking sheet or other baking pan where the biscuits can be placed wider apart, allowing air to circulate and creating a crisper exterior, and brush the pan with butter.

Fork-sift or whisk 2 cups of flour, the baking powder, and the salt in a large bowl, preferably wider than it is deep, and set aside the remaining ¼ cup of flour. Scatter the ¼-inch-size pieces of chilled fat over the flour and work in by rubbing fingers with the fat and flour as if snapping thumb and fingers together (or use two forks or knives, or a pastry cutter) until the mixture looks like well-crumbled feta cheese. Scatter the ½-inch-size pieces of chilled fat over the flour mixture and continue snapping thumb and fingers together until no pieces remain larger than a pea. Shake the bowl occasionally to allow the larger pieces of fat to bounce to the top of the flour, revealing the largest lumps that still need rubbing. If this method took longer than 5 minutes, place the bowl in the refrigerator for 5 minutes to rechill the fat.

Make a deep hollow in the center of the flour with the back of your hand. Pour ¾ cup of the milk into the hollow, reserving ¼ cup milk, and stir with a rubber spatula or large metal spoon, using broad circular strokes to quickly pull the flour into the milk. Mix just until the dry ingredients are moistened and the sticky dough begins to pull away from the sides of the bowl. If there is some flour remaining on the bottom and sides of the bowl, stir in 1 to 4 tablespoons of reserved milk, just enough to incorporate the remaining flour into the shaggy wettish dough. If the dough is too wet, use more flour when shaping.

Lightly sprinkle a board or other clean surface using some of the reserved flour. Turn the dough out onto the board and sprinkle the top lightly with flour. With floured hands, fold the dough in half, and pat dough out into a ⅓- to ½-inch-thick round, using a little additional flour only if needed. Flour again if necessary, and fold the dough in half a second time. If the dough is still clumpy, pat and fold a third time. Pat dough out into a ½-inch-thick round for a normal biscuit, ¾-inch-thick for a tall biscuit, and 1-inch-thick for a giant biscuit. Brush off any visible flour from the top. For each biscuit, dip a 2½-inch biscuit cutter into the reserved flour and cut out the biscuits, starting at the outside edge and cutting very close together, being careful not to twist the cutter. The scraps may be combined to make additional biscuits, although these scraps make tougher biscuits. For hand-shaping and other variations, see pages 24–26.

Using a metal spatula if necessary, move the biscuits to the pan or baking sheet. Bake the biscuits on the top rack of the oven for a total of 10 to 14 minutes until light golden brown. After 6 minutes, rotate the pan in the oven so that the front of the pan is now turned to the back, and check to see if the bottoms are browning too quickly. If so, slide another baking pan underneath to add insulation and retard browning. Continue baking another 4 to 8 minutes until the biscuits are light golden brown. When the biscuits are done, remove from the oven and lightly brush the tops with softened or melted butter. Turn the biscuits out upside down on a plate to cool slightly. Serve hot, right side up.

Basic Southern Biscuits

Makes 12 to 18 (2-inch) biscuits

*This very basic recipe is the standard recipe used
by most Southern families as their guide to what
a biscuit should be. If a more crumbly biscuit is
desired, increase the shortening to ¾ cup.*

2¼ cups commercial or homemade
self-rising flour (page 17), divided

¼ cup chilled shortening, lard, and/or butter,
roughly cut into ¼-inch pieces
AND
¼ cup chilled shortening, lard, and/or butter,
roughly cut into ½-inch pieces

1 cup milk or buttermilk, divided

Softened butter, for brushing

Preheat oven to 425 degrees F.

Select the baking pan by determining if a soft or crisp exterior
is desired. For a soft exterior, use an 8- or 9-inch cake pan,
pizza pan, or ovenproof skillet where the biscuits will nestle
together snugly, creating the soft exterior while baking. For
a crisp exterior, select a baking sheet or other baking pan
where the biscuits can be placed wider apart, allowing air to
circulate and creating a crisper exterior, and brush the pan
with butter.

Fork-sift or whisk 2 cups of flour in a large bowl, preferably
wider than it is deep, and set aside the remaining ¼ cup. Scatter
the ¼-inch-size pieces of chilled fat over the flour and work
in by rubbing fingers with the fat and flour as if snapping
thumb and fingers together (or use two forks or knives, or
a pastry cutter) until the mixture looks like well-crumbled
feta cheese. Scatter the ½-inch-size pieces of chilled fat over
the flour mixture and continue snapping thumb and fingers
together until no pieces remain larger than a pea. Shake the
bowl occasionally to allow the larger pieces of fat to bounce to
the top of the flour, revealing the largest lumps that still need
rubbing. If this method took longer than 5 minutes, place the
bowl in the refrigerator for 5 minutes to rechill the fat.

Make a deep hollow in the center of the flour with the back of
your hand. Pour ¾ cup of the milk into the hollow, reserving
¼ cup milk, and stir with a rubber spatula or large metal
spoon, using broad circular strokes to quickly pull the flour
into the milk. Mix just until the dry ingredients are moistened
and the sticky dough begins to pull away from the sides of the

bowl. If there is some flour remaining on the bottom and sides of the bowl, stir in 1 to 4 tablespoons of reserved milk, just enough to incorporate the remaining flour into the shaggy wettish dough. If the dough is too wet, use more flour when shaping.

Lightly sprinkle a board or other clean surface using some of the reserved flour. Turn the dough out onto the board and sprinkle the top lightly with flour. With floured hands, fold the dough in half, and pat dough out into a ⅓- to ½-inch-thick round, using a little additional flour only if needed. Flour again if necessary, and fold the dough in half a second time. If the dough is still clumpy, pat and fold a third time. Pat dough out into a ½-inch-thick round for a normal biscuit, ¾-inch-thick for a tall biscuit, and 1-inch-thick for a giant biscuit. Brush off any visible flour from the top. For each biscuit, dip a 2½-inch biscuit cutter into the reserved flour and cut out the biscuits, starting at the outside edge and cutting very close together, being careful not to twist the cutter. The scraps may be combined to make additional biscuits, although these scraps make tougher biscuits. For hand-shaping and other variations, see pages 24–26.

Using a metal spatula if necessary, move the biscuits to the pan or baking sheet. Bake the biscuits on the top rack of the oven for a total of 10 to 14 minutes until light golden brown. After 6 minutes, rotate the pan in the oven so that the front of the pan is now turned to the back, and check to see if the bottoms are browning too quickly. If so, slide another baking pan underneath to add insulation and retard browning. Continue baking another 4 to 8 minutes until the biscuits are light golden brown. When the biscuits are done, remove from the oven and lightly brush the tops with softened or melted butter. Turn the biscuits out upside down on a plate to cool slightly. Serve hot, right side up.

TIP: Shortening comes in several forms. The best kind to keep on hand for biscuits is the stick variety. It can be put in the freezer for extra chilling.

TIP: There is ½ inch between each line marked on the paper enclosing a stick of butter, margarine, or shortening. The ½-inch space between each two lines equals 1 tablespoon, or 3 teaspoons; for ½ tablespoon, or 1½ teaspoons, cut halfway between the two lines.

Novice Tea Towel Smooth-Topped Biscuits

Makes 12 (2½-inch) biscuits

For those of us who are stickiness-averse, there are all sorts of ways of shaping and kneading biscuits. The tea towel keeps the dough from sticking—coating top and bottom with flour but leaving a very smooth top and a soft inside.

3 cups commercial or homemade self-rising flour (page 17), divided

¼ cup chilled shortening, roughly cut into ¼-inch pieces
AND
¼ cup chilled shortening, roughly cut into ½-inch pieces

1 cup milk

Softened butter, for brushing

Preheat oven to 500 degrees F.

Select the baking pan by determining if a soft or crisp exterior is desired. For a soft exterior, use an 8- or 9-inch cake pan, pizza pan, or ovenproof skillet where the biscuits will nestle together snugly, creating the soft exterior while baking. For a crisp exterior, select a baking sheet or other baking pan where the biscuits can be placed wider apart, allowing air to circulate and creating a crisper exterior, and brush the pan with butter.

Fork-sift or whisk 2½ cups of flour in a large bowl, preferably wider than it is deep, and set aside the remaining ½ cup. Scatter the ¼-inch-size pieces of chilled fat over the flour and work in by rubbing fingers with the fat and flour as if snapping thumb and fingers together (or use two forks or knives, or a pastry cutter) until the mixture looks like well-crumbled feta cheese. Scatter the ½-inch-size pieces of chilled fat over the flour mixture and continue snapping thumb and fingers together until no pieces remain larger than a pea. Shake the bowl occasionally to allow the larger pieces of fat to bounce to the top of the flour, revealing the largest lumps that still need rubbing. If this method took longer than 5 minutes, place the bowl in the refrigerator for 5 minutes to rechill the fat.

Make a deep hollow in the center of the flour with the back of your hand. Pour the milk into the hollow and stir with a rubber spatula or large metal spoon, using broad circular strokes to quickly pull the flour into the milk. Mix just until the dry ingredients are moistened and the sticky dough begins to pull away from the sides of the bowl. This is a very wet dough.

Spread a clean tea towel or a kitchen towel on a board or table and sprinkle ⅓ cup of reserved flour. Turn the dough out onto the center of the floured towel. Pick the dough up and turn it in the flour a few times to lightly coat the outside, then place the dough to the left or right of the center of the towel. Fold the floured towel over the top of the dough. With your hands or a rolling pin, pat or roll the outside of the towel lightly until the dough is flattened to ½ inch thick. Open the towel. The dough should be smooth, coated with flour on the outside, and wet on the inside.

Working from the outside edge in, frequently dip a 2½-inch biscuit cutter into the remaining flour and cut out the biscuits without twisting. The scraps may be combined to make additional biscuits, although these scraps make tougher biscuits. Brush the flour off the biscuits with a pastry brush if desired.

Using a metal spatula if necessary, move the biscuits to the pan or baking sheet. Bake the biscuits on the top rack of the oven for a total of 10 to 12 minutes until light golden brown. After 5 minutes, rotate the pan in the oven so that the front of the pan is now turned to the back, and check to see if the bottoms are browning too quickly. If so, slide another baking pan underneath to add insulation and retard browning. Continue baking another 5 to 7 minutes until the biscuits are light golden brown. When the biscuits are done, lightly brush the tops with melted butter. Turn the biscuits out upside down on a plate to cool slightly. Serve hot, right side up.

Try using the novice tea towel method.

Hand-Rolled Extra-Light Biscuits

Makes 12 biscuits

You'll get a lighter biscuit if you learn to hand-roll. Give yourself permission to practice with several batches.

2¼ cups all-purpose flour, divided

1 tablespoon baking powder

1 teaspoon salt

¼ cup chilled shortening, lard, and/or butter, roughly cut into ¼-inch pieces
AND
¼ cup chilled shortening, lard, and/or butter, roughly cut into ½-inch pieces

1¼ cup milk or buttermilk, divided

Softened butter, for brushing

Preheat oven to 425 degrees F.

Select the baking pan by determining if a soft or crisp exterior is desired. For a soft exterior, use an 8- or 9-inch cake pan, pizza pan, or ovenproof skillet where the biscuits will nestle together snugly, creating the soft exterior while baking. For a crisp exterior, select a baking sheet or other baking pan where the biscuits can be placed wider apart, allowing air to circulate and creating a crisper exterior, and brush the pan with butter.

Fork-sift or whisk 2 cups of flour, baking powder, and salt in a large bowl, preferably wider than it is deep, and set aside the remaining ¼ cup of flour. Scatter the ¼-inch-size pieces of chilled fat over the flour and work in by rubbing fingers with the fat and flour as if snapping thumb and fingers together (or use two forks or knives, or a pastry cutter) until the mixture looks like well-crumbled feta cheese. Scatter the ½-inch-size pieces of chilled fat over the flour mixture and continue snapping thumb and fingers together until no pieces remain larger than a pea. Shake the bowl occasionally to allow the larger pieces of fat to bounce to the top of the flour, revealing the largest lumps that still need rubbing. If this method took longer than 5 minutes, place the bowl in the refrigerator for 5 minutes to rechill the fat.

Make a deep hollow in the center of the flour with the back of your hand. Pour 1 cup of the milk into the hollow, reserving ¼ cup milk, and stir with a rubber spatula or large metal spoon, using broad circular strokes to quickly pull the flour into the milk. Mix just until the dry ingredients are moistened and the sticky dough begins to pull away from the sides of the bowl. If there is some flour remaining on the bottom and sides of the bowl, stir in 1 to 4 tablespoons of reserved milk, just enough to incorporate the remaining flour into the shaggy wettish dough. If the dough is too wet, use more flour when shaping.

Lightly sprinkle a board or other clean surface using some of the reserved flour. Turn the dough out onto the board and sprinkle the top lightly with flour. Divide the dough into 4 equal pieces using a sharp knife or pastry cutter. Divide each piece into 3 smaller portions. With floured hands, hold one of the 12 small pieces of dough gently in one hand. Cup your other hand over the biscuit and roll the dough around several times in the palm of the other, using thumb and pinkie fingers to rotate the biscuit, until the top of the biscuit is smoothed by the top palm, the bottom smoothed by bottom palm.

Move the biscuits to the pan or baking sheet. Bake them on the top rack of the oven for a total of 10 to 14 minutes until light golden brown. After 6 minutes, rotate the pan in the oven so that the front of the pan is now turned to the back, and check to see if the bottoms are browning too quickly. If so, slide another baking pan underneath to add insulation and retard browning. Continue baking another 4 to 8 minutes until the biscuits are light golden brown. When the biscuits are done, remove from the oven and lightly brush the tops with softened or melted butter. Turn the biscuits out upside down on a plate to cool slightly. Serve hot, right side up.

Kate's Unforgettable Wooden Bowl Biscuits

The method of making biscuits in a traditional wooden bowl, without a recipe, was traditionally practiced by home cooks all over the South. A sack of flour was emptied into the bowl, a well was made in the flour, and then the number of biscuits desired was miraculously shaped by the addition of fat and liquid. The remaining flour mixture was then sifted and returned to the bowl, covered with a tea towel or flour sack, or to the sack itself until the biscuits were made again later in the day.

Alas, this process is so intimidating to novice cooks, until they get the "feel," that I have to caution the novice to try another recipe first. Please come back and try these after practicing with easier versions, because this version makes biscuits the way they are supposed to be—meltingly light, tantalizingly tender, flaky, moist—and unforgettable. I have never had a better biscuit than Kate's.

1 (5-pound) bag self-rising flour,
to use 2½ cups flour

1 portion sweet (fresh) milk, approximately 1 cup

1 handful chilled lard, hard shortening,
or butter, approximately ⅓–½ cup

Softened butter, for brushing

Preheat oven to 500 degrees F.

Fill a wooden biscuit bowl ⅔ full with as much of the bag of flour as possible. Use the back of a hand to form and simultaneously pack an 8-inch well in the center of the flour, leaving a small amount on the bottom. Gently pour the milk into the well-packed center of the well. Scoop ⅓ cup of room-temperature lard into the milk. Using the fingers of one hand, mush together the milk and fat until it looks like thick lumpy pancake batter. Making a massaging motion with the fingers of one hand, slightly akin to playing the scales on a banjo, move the batter around the well in a whirlpool. Continue moving the fingers steadily around the bowl as a rotary mixer would, like a centrifuge. The batter will gently pull in the packed flour. After a few rotations, it will have pulled in sufficient flour to make a very wet dough in the center of the bowl, cradled by the rest of the flour.

Re-flour both hands in the remaining flour and scrape the wet mess off the gooey hand back into the dough. Re-flour both hands and slide under the dough, turning it completely over in the remaining flour with the wet portion of the flour at the bottom of the dough and the top portion completely floured. Re-flouring hands as needed, pinch off an egg-sized portion of the dough sufficient for a 1½-inch biscuit. The portion pulled from the dough will be wet. Dip it into the flour so the total exterior of the dough is now floured. Cup one hand, making sure the palm is floured, and move the dough on top of the palm. Use the palm of the second hand to smooth the top of the dough with pinkie and thumb to keep it round. Using a metal spatula if necessary, move biscuit to an iron skillet or small baking sheet. Repeat with subsequent biscuits, nestling close to each other to keep upright. When pan is full and dough is all used, re-sift flour into the bowl, discarding any pieces of dough left in the sifter, and cover flour with a clean tea towel to use the next day.

Bake the biscuits on the top rack of the oven for a total of 10 to 14 minutes until light golden brown. After 6 minutes, rotate the pan in the oven so that the front of the pan is now turned to the back, and check to see if the bottoms are browning too quickly. If so, slide another baking pan underneath to add insulation and retard browning. Continue baking another 4 to 8 minutes until the biscuits are light golden brown. When the biscuits are done, remove from the oven and lightly brush the tops with softened or melted butter. Turn the biscuits out upside down on a plate to cool slightly. Serve hot, right side up.

WOODEN BOWLS

Wooden bowls are the easiest place to make biscuits. They are large and shallow enough to allow the sweeping motion required, combining the ingredients without spilling flour everywhere; and if used regularly, they don't require washing. Any remaining dough scrapes out easily, the bowl is wiped out, and it's ready for another batch.

Mishap Skillet Biscuits

Makes 8 biscuit wedges

They say necessity is the mother of invention. Whoever "they" are, they are wrong. I find that mistakes are the mother of invention. What began as Shirley Corriher's biscuit recipe from a book, rapidly evolved into something tender and cakey with each fumbled measurement and misread ingredient. Dumping the dough into a cast-iron skillet resulted in an incredibly light, ethereal biscuit. While it is pleasantly delicate, it does not give that same hearty and fulfilling mouth feel that traditional biscuits do. See Shirley Corriher's Country Buttermilk Biscuits (page 65) for her current technique and measurements. They're also delicious.

2¼ cups commercial or homemade
self-rising flour (page 17), divided

½ teaspoon salt

⅓ cup heavy cream

1¼ cups buttermilk, divided

Softened butter, for brushing

Preheat oven to 425 degrees F. Butter a 9-inch cast-iron skillet and set aside.

Fork-sift or whisk 2 cups of flour and the salt in a large bowl, preferably wider than it is deep, and set aside the remaining ¼ cup of flour.

Make a deep hollow in the center of the flour with the back of your hand. Pour the cream and 1 cup of buttermilk into the hollow, reserving the remaining ¼ cup of buttermilk, and stir with a rubber spatula or large metal spoon, using broad circular strokes to quickly pull the flour into the liquid. Mix just until the dry ingredients are moistened and the sticky dough begins to pull away from the sides of the bowl. If there is some flour remaining on the bottom and sides of the bowl, stir in 1 to 4 tablespoons of reserved buttermilk, just enough to incorporate the remaining flour into the shaggy wettish dough. If the dough is too wet, use more flour when shaping.

Turn the dough out into the prepared skillet and pat the top so it's even. Score the dough into eight wedges, not cutting all the way through. Bake on the top rack of the oven for 20 minutes, or until the biscuit is lightly browned and firm to the touch. Take care as they will brown faster on the bottom when made in a dark skillet. Brush with melted butter, cut into wedges, and serve warm.

Shirley Corriher's Country Buttermilk Biscuits

Makes 12 to 18 (2-inch) biscuits

Shirley has taught countless people to make biscuits, in part because they are delicious and in part because she makes it look so easy. She learned to make biscuits at her grandmother's knee, but she kind of forgot until she came to Rich's Cooking School. It dawned on Shirley while watching Kate Almand shape her wet dough that her Nanny's biscuits were also wet. The light went on and Shirley was able to "get her granny's touch" back. She has changed her recipe over the years, and this is the current one on the back of Midstate Mills Tenda-Bake Self-Rising Flour bag.

2 cups commercial or homemade self-rising flour (page 17)

¼ cup granulated sugar

½ teaspoon salt

¼ cup chilled shortening or lard, roughly cut into ½-inch pieces

⅔ cup heavy cream

¾ cup buttermilk

1 cup all-purpose flour, for shaping

2 tablespoons unsalted butter, melted

Preheat oven to 425 degrees F with the rack placed above the middle of the oven.

Grease a 9-inch round cake pan or spray with nonstick spray if not seasoned.

Combine the self-rising flour, sugar, and salt. Work shortening in with your fingers until there are no large lumps. Stir in cream and then buttermilk until it resembles cottage cheese (very sticky). Add more buttermilk if needed. Spread all-purpose flour in a shallow pan. Scoop dough (use a #30 ice cream scoop) into flour, leaving space between each. Coat with flour. Gently shape into a round, shaking off excess flour. Place the biscuit into the prepared pan smooched up against its neighbor. Continue scooping and shaping. Bake until light brown for 20 to 25 minutes. Brush with melted butter. Invert onto a plate, back onto another. Cut biscuits apart to serve.

Biscuits Supreme

Makes 12 (2½-inch) biscuits

Better Homes and Gardens has produced some excellent cookbooks, and this is an old recipe adapted from one of them. Rich buttery biscuits lack the tenderness of lard and shortening but make up for it with their flavor and flakiness.

2¼ cups all-purpose flour, divided

½ tablespoon baking powder

2 teaspoons granulated sugar

½ teaspoon salt

½ teaspoon cream of tartar

½ cup chilled butter, or ¼ cup chilled butter and ¼ cup chilled shortening, roughly cut into ½-inch pieces

1 cup milk, divided

Softened butter, for brushing

Preheat oven to 450 degrees F.

Select the baking pan by determining if a soft or crisp exterior is desired. For a soft exterior, use an 8- or 9-inch cake pan, pizza pan, or ovenproof skillet where the biscuits will nestle together snugly, creating the soft exterior while baking. For a crisp exterior, select a baking sheet or other baking pan where the biscuits can be placed wider apart, allowing air to circulate and creating a crisper exterior, and brush the pan with butter.

Fork-sift or whisk 2 cups of flour, baking powder, sugar, salt, and cream of tartar in a large bowl, preferably wider than it is deep, and set aside the remaining ¼ cup of flour. Scatter the pieces of chilled butter over the flour and work in by rubbing your fingers with the butter and flour as if snapping your thumb and fingers together (or use two forks or knives, or a pastry cutter) until the mixture looks like well-crumbled feta cheese, with no piece larger than a pea. Shake the bowl occasionally to allow the larger pieces of fat to bounce to the top of the flour, revealing the largest lumps that still need rubbing. If this method took longer than 5 minutes, place the bowl in the refrigerator for 5 minutes to rechill the fat.

Make a deep hollow in the center of the flour with the back of your hand. Pour ¾ cup of milk into the hollow, reserving remaining ¼ cup, and stir with a rubber spatula or large metal spoon, using broad circular strokes to quickly pull the flour into the milk. Mix just until the dry ingredients are moistened and the sticky dough begins to pull away from the sides of the bowl. If there is some flour remaining on the bottom and sides of the bowl, stir in 1 to 4 tablespoons of reserved milk, just enough to incorporate the remaining flour into the shaggy wettish dough. If the dough is too wet, use more flour when shaping.

Lightly sprinkle a board or other clean surface using some of the reserved flour. Turn the dough out onto the board and sprinkle the top lightly with flour. With floured hands, fold the dough in half, and pat dough out into a ⅓- to ½-inch-thick round, using a little additional flour only if needed. Flour again if necessary, and fold the dough in half a second time. If the dough is still clumpy, pat and fold a third time. Pat dough out into a ½-inch-thick round for a normal biscuit, ¾-inch-thick for a tall biscuit, and 1-inch-thick for a giant biscuit. Brush off any visible flour from the top. For each biscuit, dip a 2½-inch biscuit cutter into the reserved flour and cut out the biscuits, starting at the outside edge and cutting very close together, being careful not to twist the cutter. The scraps may be combined to make additional biscuits, although these scraps make tougher biscuits. For hand-shaping and other variations, see pages 24–26.

Using a metal spatula if necessary, move the biscuits to the pan or baking sheet. Bake the biscuits on the top rack of the oven for a total of 10 to 14 minutes until light golden brown. After 6 minutes, rotate the pan in the oven so that the front of the pan is now turned to the back, and check to see if the bottoms are browning

CREAM OF TARTAR

Cream of tartar is a fine white powder that is used as an acid in some baking powders and has less aftertaste than baking soda.

too quickly. If so, slide another baking pan underneath to add insulation and retard browning. Continue baking another 4 to 8 minutes until the biscuits are light golden brown. When the biscuits are done, remove from the oven and lightly brush the tops with softened or melted butter. Turn the biscuits out upside down on a plate to cool slightly. Serve hot, right side up.

"Bomber" Biscuits

Makes 2 to 4 (4-inch) biscuits

This recipe is adapted from a charming book titled At Home Café *by Helen DeFrance and Leslie Carpenter. "Bomber" Biscuits are huge enough to satisfy any appetite, breakfast, lunch, or dinner, and are particularly pleasing to children of all ages. Having a biscuit mix of one's own already made in the refrigerator is a speedy way to make them.*

2 cups Homemade Refrigerator Biscuit Mix (page 50) or commercial biscuit mix

½ cup sour cream

½ cup club soda, divided

¼ cup all-purpose flour

¼ cup butter, melted

Confectioners' sugar, optional

Preheat oven to 450 degrees F.

Select the baking pan by determining if a soft or crisp exterior is desired. For a soft exterior, use an 8- or 9-inch cake pan, pizza pan, or ovenproof skillet where the biscuits will nestle together snugly, creating the soft exterior while baking. For a crisp exterior, select a baking sheet or other baking pan where the biscuits can be placed wider apart, allowing air to circulate and creating a crisper exterior, and brush the pan with butter.

Fork-sift or whisk the biscuit mix in a large bowl, preferably wider than it is deep. Make a deep hollow in the center of the mix with the back of your hand. Combine the sour cream and ¼ cup of the club soda in a small bowl. Pour the sour cream mixture into the hollow and stir with a rubber spatula or large metal spoon, using broad circular strokes to quickly pull the flour into the liquids. Add the remaining club soda and mix just until the dry ingredients are moistened and the sticky dough begins to pull away from the sides of the bowl. If there is some flour remaining in the bottom and sides of the bowl, stir in 1 to 4 tablespoons of water, just enough to incorporate the remaining flour into the shaggy wettish dough.

Lightly sprinkle a board or other clean surface using the all-purpose flour. Turn the dough out onto the board and sprinkle the top lightly with flour. With floured hands, fold the dough in half, and pat dough out into a ⅓- to ½-inch-thick round, using a little additional flour only if needed. Flour again if necessary, and fold the dough in half a second time. If the dough is still clumpy, pat and fold a third time. Pat dough out into a ½-inch-thick round for a normal biscuit, ¾-inch-thick for a tall biscuit, and 1-inch-thick for a giant biscuit. Brush off any visible flour from the top. For each biscuit, dip a 4-inch biscuit cutter into the reserved flour and cut out the biscuits, starting at the outside edge and cutting very close together, being careful not to twist the cutter. The scraps may be combined to make additional biscuits, although these scraps make tougher biscuits. For hand-shaping and other variations, see pages 24–26.

Using a metal spatula if necessary, move the biscuits to the pan or baking sheet. Bake the biscuits on the top rack of the oven for a total 14 to 17 minutes until light golden brown. After 7 minutes, rotate the pan in the oven so that the front of the pan is now turned to the back, and check to see if the bottoms are browning too quickly. If so, slide another baking pan underneath to add insulation and retard browning. Continue baking another 6 to 10 minutes until the biscuits are light golden brown. When the biscuits are done, remove from the oven and lightly brush the tops with softened or melted butter. Turn the biscuits out upside down on a plate to cool slightly. Serve hot, right side up. Dust the tops of the biscuits with confectioners' sugar if desired.

Bumpy-Topped Mock Clabber Biscuits

Makes 18 (2-inch) biscuits

Before pasteurization and homogenization, when milk was delivered to each home and left on the doorstep or perhaps in a minimally insulated milk box on the back porch, I sometimes neglected to bring in the milk during the summer, preferring to play with my friends; by the time my mother came home, it would have soured the cream, pushing its way up to the top of the glass bottle, perhaps even pushing off the top. It would fall to me to clean up the mess. We didn't have much money, so methods were derived to use even the soured milk. When making buttermilk and clabber, cream rises to the top and is used as is, or it's made into butter. It's impossible to clabber pasteurized milk, but the sour cream and commercial buttermilk give a similar taste here. Cynthia and my grandmother enjoyed the top cream, Cynthia for tea and my grandmother for coffee. Both were cross when homogenized milk became the standard.

2½ cups all-purpose flour, divided

4 teaspoons baking powder

½ teaspoon baking soda

1 teaspoon salt

⅓ cup chilled butter, roughly
cut into ½-inch pieces

1¾ cup sour cream, divided

Preheat oven to 425 degrees F.

Select the baking pan by determining if a soft or crisp exterior is desired. For a soft exterior, use an 8- or 9-inch cake pan, pizza pan, or ovenproof skillet where the biscuits will nestle together snugly, creating the soft exterior while baking. For a crisp exterior, select a baking sheet or other baking pan where the biscuits can be placed wider apart, allowing air to circulate and creating a crisper exterior, and brush the pan with butter.

Fork-sift or whisk 2¼ cups of the flour, baking powder, baking soda, and salt in a large bowl, preferably wider than it is deep, and set aside the remaining ¼ cup of flour. Scatter the pieces of chilled butter over the flour and work in by rubbing fingers with the butter and flour as if snapping thumb and fingers together (or use two forks or knives, or a pastry cutter) until the mixture looks like well-crumbled feta cheese, with no piece larger than a pea. Shake the bowl occasionally to allow the larger pieces of fat to bounce to the top of the flour, revealing the largest lumps that still need rubbing. If this method took longer than 5 minutes, place the bowl in the refrigerator for 5 minutes to rechill the fat.

Make a deep hollow in the center of the flour with the back of your hand. Pour 1½ cups of the sour cream into the hollow, reserving ¼ cup. Stir the sour cream, using broad circular strokes to quickly pull the flour into the sour cream. Mix just until the dry ingredients are moistened and the sticky dough begins to pull away from the sides of the bowl. If there is some flour remaining in the bottom and sides of the bowl, stir in 1 to 4 tablespoons of reserved sour cream, just enough to incorporate the remaining flour into the shaggy wettish dough. If the dough is too wet, use more flour when shaping.

Lightly sprinkle a board or other clean surface using some of the reserved flour. Turn the dough out onto the board and sprinkle the top of the dough lightly with flour. With floured hands, fold the dough in half, and pat dough out into a ⅓- to ½-inch-thick round, using a little additional flour only if needed. Flour again if necessary, and fold the dough in half a second time. If the dough is still clumpy, pat and fold a third time. Pat dough out into a ½-inch-thick round for a normal biscuit, ¾-inch-thick for a tall biscuit, and 1-inch-thick for a giant biscuit. Brush off any visible flour from the top. For each biscuit, dip a 2-inch biscuit cutter into the reserved flour and cut out the biscuits, starting at the outside edge and cutting very close together, being careful not to twist the cutter. The scraps may be combined to make additional biscuits, although these scraps make tougher biscuits. For hand-shaping and other variations, see pages 24–26.

Using a metal spatula if necessary, move the biscuits to the pan or baking sheet. Bake the biscuits on the top rack of the oven for a total 10 to 14 minutes, until light golden brown. After 6 minutes, rotate the pan in the oven so that the front of the pan is now turned to the back, and check to see if the bottoms are browning too quickly. If so, slide another baking pan underneath to add insulation and retard browning. Continue baking another 4 to 8 minutes, until the biscuits are light golden brown. When the biscuits are done, remove from the oven and lightly brush the top of the biscuits with softened or melted butter. Turn the biscuits out upside down on a plate to cool slightly. Serve hot, right side up.

VARIATION: CHEESE BISCUITS

Add ½ cup cheddar cheese; for an herb biscuit, add 1 tablespoon of your favorite fresh herbs such as chopped basil or thyme.

James Villas' Maw-Maw's Biscuits

Makes 20 biscuits

Adapted from the Clabber Biscuits of his grandmother's in James Villas' My Mother's Southern Kitchen, this is one of our top favorite biscuits, with a lovely downiness and just enough tartness to intrigue, mixed with an incredibly buttery finish of flavor. It is an exceptional biscuit, much like a clabbered biscuit, and worth keeping the recipe handy. A few hours of chilling these, but not much longer, will give an even better biscuit with even more rise.

2¾ cups all-purpose flour, divided

4 teaspoons baking powder

1 teaspoon baking soda

1 teaspoon salt

⅓ cup chilled butter, roughly cut into ½-inch pieces

1¾ cup sour cream, divided

Softened butter, for brushing

Preheat oven to 425 degrees F.

Select the baking pan by determining if a soft or crisp exterior is desired. For a soft exterior, use an 8- or 9-inch cake pan, pizza pan, or ovenproof skillet where the biscuits will nestle together snugly, creating the soft exterior while baking. For a crisp exterior, select a baking sheet or other baking pan where the biscuits can be placed wider apart, allowing air to circulate and creating a crisper exterior, and brush the pan with butter.

Fork-sift or whisk 2½ cups of the flour, baking powder, baking soda, and salt in a large bowl, preferably wider than it is deep, and set aside the remaining ¼ cup of flour. Scatter the pieces of chilled butter over the flour and work in by rubbing fingers with the butter and flour as if snapping thumb and fingers together (or use two forks or knives, or a pastry cutter) until the mixture looks like well-crumbled feta cheese, with no piece larger than a pea. Shake the bowl occasionally to allow the larger pieces of fat to bounce to the top of the flour, revealing the largest lumps that still need rubbing. If this method took longer than 5 minutes, place the bowl in the refrigerator for 5 minutes to rechill the fat.

Make a deep hollow in the center of the flour with the back of your hand. Pour 1½ cups of the sour cream into the hollow, reserving ¼ cup sour cream, and stir the sour cream, using broad circular strokes to quickly pull the flour into the sour cream. Mix just until the dry ingredients are moistened and the sticky dough begins to pull away from the sides of the bowl. If there is some flour remaining in the bottom and sides of the bowl, stir in 1 to 4 tablespoons of reserved sour cream, just enough to incorporate the remaining flour into the shaggy wettish dough. If the dough is too wet, use more flour when shaping.

Lightly sprinkle a board or other clean surface using some of the reserved flour. Turn the dough out onto the board and sprinkle the top of the dough lightly with flour. With floured hands, fold the dough in half, and pat dough out into a ⅓- to ½-inch-thick round, using a little additional flour only if needed. Flour again if necessary, and fold the dough in half a second time. If the dough is still clumpy, pat and fold a third time. Pat dough out into a ½-inch-thick round for a normal biscuit, ¾-inch-thick for a tall biscuit, and 1-inch-thick for a giant biscuit. Brush off any visible flour from the top. For each biscuit, dip a 2½-inch biscuit cutter into the reserved flour and cut out the biscuits, starting at the outside edge and cutting very close together, being careful not to twist the cutter. The scraps may be combined to make additional biscuits, although these scraps make tougher biscuits. For hand-shaping and other variations, see pages 24–26.

Using a metal spatula if necessary, move the biscuits to the pan or baking sheet. Bake the biscuits on the top rack of the oven for a total of 10 to 14 minutes, until light golden brown. After 6 minutes, rotate the pan in the oven so that the front of the pan is now turned to the back, and check to see if the bottoms are browning too quickly. If so, slide another baking pan underneath to add insulation and retard browning. Continue baking another 4 to 8 minutes, until the biscuits are light golden brown. When the biscuits are done, remove from the oven and lightly brush the top of the biscuits with softened or melted butter. Turn the biscuits out upside down on a plate to cool slightly. Serve hot, right side up.

Double Fluffy Buttermilk Biscuits

Makes 14 (2½-inch) biscuits

After an interruption once when cooking, an additional ¼ cup of fat was inadvertently added to a recipe. Finding that the result yielded a biscuit with added height, fluff, and tenderness made it easy to decide to keep this delicious "mistake."

2¼ cups commercial or homemade self-rising flour (page 17), divided

¼ cup chilled shortening, roughly cut into ¼-inch pieces
AND
¼ cup chilled shortening, roughly cut into ½-inch pieces

1¼ cup buttermilk (or 1¼ cup milk plus 1 tablespoon lemon juice), divided

Softened butter, for brushing

Preheat oven to 400 degrees F.

Select the baking pan by determining if a soft or crisp exterior is desired. For a soft exterior, use an 8- or 9-inch cake pan, pizza pan, or ovenproof skillet where the biscuits will nestle together snugly, creating the soft exterior while baking. For a crisp exterior, select a baking sheet or other baking pan where the biscuits can be placed wider apart, allowing air to circulate and creating a crisper exterior, and brush the pan with butter.

Fork-sift or whisk 2 cups of flour in a large bowl, preferably wider than it is deep, and set aside the remaining ¼ cup of flour. Scatter the ¼-inch-size pieces of chilled shortening over the flour and work in by rubbing fingers with the fat and flour as if snapping thumb and fingers together (or use two forks or knives, or a pastry cutter) until the mixture looks like well-crumbled feta cheese. Scatter the ½-inch-size pieces of chilled fat over the flour mixture and continue snapping thumb and fingers together until no pieces remain larger than a pea. Shake the bowl occasionally to allow the larger pieces of fat to bounce to the top of the flour, revealing the largest lumps that still need rubbing. If this method took longer than 5 minutes, place the bowl in the refrigerator for 5 minutes to rechill the fat.

Make a deep hollow in the center of the flour with the back of your hand. Pour 1 cup of the buttermilk into the hollow, reserving ¼ cup buttermilk, and stir with a rubber spatula or large metal spoon, using broad circular strokes to quickly pull the flour into the buttermilk. Mix just until the dry ingredients are moistened and the sticky dough begins to pull away from the sides of the bowl. If there is some flour remaining on the bottom and sides of the bowl, stir in 1 to 4 tablespoons of reserved buttermilk, just enough to incorporate the remaining flour into the shaggy wettish dough. If the dough is too wet, use more flour when shaping.

Lightly sprinkle a board or other clean surface using some of the reserved flour. Turn the dough out onto the board and sprinkle the top lightly with flour. With floured hands, fold the dough in half, and pat dough out into a 1/3- to 1/2-inch-thick round, using a little additional flour only if needed. Flour again if necessary, and fold the dough in half a second time. If the dough is still clumpy, pat and fold a third time. Pat dough out into a 1/2-inch-thick round for a normal biscuit, 3/4-inch-thick for a tall biscuit, and 1-inch-thick for a giant biscuit. Brush off any visible flour from the top. For each biscuit, dip a 2 1/2-inch biscuit cutter into the reserved flour and cut out the biscuits, starting at the outside edge and cutting very close together, being careful not to twist the cutter. The scraps may be combined to make additional biscuits, although these scraps make tougher biscuits. For hand-shaping and other variations, see pages 24–26.

Using a metal spatula if necessary, move the biscuits to the pan or baking sheet. Bake the biscuits on the top rack of the oven for a total of 10 to 14 minutes until light golden brown. After 6 minutes, rotate the pan in the oven so that the front of the pan is now turned to the back, and check to see if the bottoms are browning too quickly. If so, slide another baking pan underneath to add insulation and retard browning. Continue baking another 4 to 8 minutes until the biscuits are light golden brown. When the biscuits are done, remove from the oven and lightly brush the tops with softened or melted butter. Turn the biscuits out upside down on a plate to cool slightly. Serve hot, right side up.

VARIATION: GEORGIA SORGHUM BISCUITS

Replace 1/4 cup of the buttermilk with sorghum.

Food Processor Biscuits

Makes 12 to 18 (2½-inch) biscuits

There are many ways of making food processor biscuits. Some people prefer processing the cold fat with the flour with a few pulses until it is pea-sized, then moving it to a bowl and stirring in the liquid. That is just too much bother for me—and makes too many messes—first the food processor, then the bowl, and then the work surface where it is shaped. A tender biscuit should not be overworked, but the liquid does need to be incorporated. It also works for me to cut in the fat and the milk together. That avoids overprocessing the fat, leaving part of the fat in large pieces and the other part cut in thoroughly, providing a tender biscuit with a good rise. Novice biscuit makers should learn to make biscuits by one of the other methods. Once they know how the dough should feel, the food processor method will be easier, and worth trying for those in a hurry.

**2½ cups commercial or homemade
self-rising flour (page 17), divided**

**¼ cup chilled shortening, lard, and/or butter,
roughly cut into ¼-inch pieces
AND
¼ cup chilled shortening, lard, and/or butter,
roughly cut into ½-inch pieces**

1 cup buttermilk or milk, divided

Softened butter, for brushing

Preheat oven to 450 degrees F.

Select the baking pan by determining if a soft or crisp exterior is desired. For a soft exterior, use an 8- or 9-inch cake pan, pizza pan, or ovenproof skillet where the biscuits will nestle together snugly, creating the soft exterior while baking. For a crisp exterior, select a baking sheet or other baking pan where the biscuits can be placed wider apart, allowing air to circulate and creating a crisper exterior, and brush the pan with butter.

Pulse 2¼ cups of flour two or three times in a food processor fitted with the knife or dough blade; set aside the remaining ¼ cup. Scatter the chilled ¼-inch shortening pieces over the flour mixture and pulse 2 or 3 times. Scatter the chilled ½-inch shortening pieces over the flour mixture and pulse 2 or 3 times until mixture resembles well-crumbled feta cheese, with no piece larger than a pea. Add ¾ cup of buttermilk, reserving the remaining ¼ cup, and pulse briefly to incorporate into a shaggy wettish dough. When the blade stops, remove the lid and feel the dough. Add more reserved liquid or flour as needed to make a slightly wettish dough. Pulse a time or two more until the dough looks shaggy but together.

Pulse until mixture resembles well-crumbled feta cheese.

Add flour if too wet.

Lightly sprinkle a board or other clean surface using some of the reserved flour. Turn the dough out onto the board and sprinkle the top lightly with flour. With floured hands, fold the dough in half, and pat dough out into a ⅓- to ½-inch-thick round, using a little additional flour only if needed. Flour again if necessary, and fold the dough in half a second time. If the dough is still clumpy, pat and fold a third time. Pat dough out into a ½-inch-thick round for a normal biscuit, ¾-inch-thick for a tall biscuit, and 1-inch-thick for a giant biscuit. Brush off any visible flour from the top. For each biscuit, dip a 2½-inch biscuit cutter into the reserved flour and cut out the biscuits, starting at the outside edge and cutting very close together, being careful not to twist the cutter. The scraps may be combined to make additional biscuits, although these scraps make tougher biscuits. For hand-shaping and other variations, see pages 24–26.

Using a metal spatula if necessary, move the biscuits to the pan or baking sheet. Bake the biscuits on the top rack of the oven for a total 10 to 14 minutes until light golden brown. After 6 minutes, rotate the pan in the oven so that the front of the pan is now turned to the back, and check to see if the bottoms are browning too quickly. If so, slide another baking pan underneath to add insulation and retard browning. Continue baking another 4 to 8 minutes until the biscuits are light golden brown. When the biscuits are done, lightly brush the tops with melted butter. Turn the biscuits out upside down on a plate to cool slightly. Serve hot, right side up.

VARIATION: I've used this technique with a mixture of half shortening and half butter, cutting the shortening in first with a few pulses, then adding the cut-up butter and ½ cup of milk, and following the directions above.

VARIATION: This is an excellent biscuit made with goat milk butter and goat milk.

VARIATION: FOOD PROCESSOR GOLDEN CHEESE BISCUITS

Pulse ½ cup shredded cheddar cheese with the mixture before adding the milk.

Fast-Food Biscuits

Makes 12 (2-inch) biscuits

For those of you who find yourself craving that buttery Hardee's or Bojangle's biscuit on your way to work in the morning, this is the biscuit for you. These puffed biscuits are more tender than other butter-based biscuits, but they are milder in flavor with a nice, crispy crust on the bottom that would be the perfect foil for a crunchy piece of bacon sandwiched in between. We usually interchange buttermilk and milk when using self-rising flour, but in this case, the buttermilk is really necessary because of the high quantity of butter. Most people who love fast-food biscuits roll this dough ¾ inch or 1 inch thick, which makes fewer biscuits.

2½ cups commercial or homemade
self-rising flour (page 17), divided

¼ cup chilled butter, roughly
cut into ¼-inch pieces
AND
¼ cup chilled butter, roughly
cut into ½-inch pieces

1¾ cups buttermilk, divided

Softened butter, for brushing

Preheat oven to 450 degrees F.

Select the baking pan by determining if a soft or crisp exterior is desired. For a soft exterior, use an 8- or 9-inch cake pan, pizza pan, or ovenproof skillet where the biscuits will nestle together snugly, creating the soft exterior while baking. For a crisp exterior, select a baking sheet or other baking pan where the biscuits can be placed wider apart, allowing air to circulate and creating a crisper exterior, and brush the pan with butter.

Fork-sift or whisk 2¼ cups of flour in a large bowl, preferably wider than it is deep, and set aside the remaining ¼ cup. Scatter the ¼-inch-size pieces of chilled fat over the flour and work in by rubbing fingers with the fat and flour as if snapping thumb and fingers together (or use two forks or knives, or a pastry cutter) until the mixture looks like well-crumbled feta cheese. Scatter the ½-inch-size pieces of chilled fat over the flour mixture and continue snapping thumb and fingers together until no pieces remain larger than a pea. Shake the bowl occasionally to allow the larger pieces of fat to bounce to the top of the flour, revealing the largest lumps that still need rubbing. If this method took longer than 5 minutes, place the bowl in the refrigerator for 5 minutes to rechill the fat.

Make a deep hollow in the center of the flour with the back of your hand. Pour 1½ cups of the buttermilk into the hollow, reserving ¼ cup, and stir with a rubber spatula or large metal spoon, using broad circular strokes to quickly pull the flour into the buttermilk. Mix just until the dry ingredients are moistened and the sticky dough begins to pull away from the sides of the bowl. If there is some flour remaining in the bottom and sides of the bowl, stir in 1 to 4 tablespoons of reserved buttermilk, just enough to incorporate the remaining flour into the shaggy wettish dough. If the dough is too wet, use more flour when shaping.

Lightly sprinkle a board or other clean surface using some of the reserved flour. Turn the dough out onto the board and sprinkle the tops lightly with flour. With floured hands, fold the dough in half, and pat dough out into a ⅓- to ½-inch-thick round, using a little additional flour only if needed. Flour again if necessary, and fold the dough in half a second time. If the dough is still clumpy, pat and fold a third time. Pat dough out into a ½-inch-thick round for a normal biscuit, ¾-inch-thick for a tall biscuit, and 1-inch-thick for a giant biscuit. Brush off any visible flour from the top. For each biscuit, dip a 2-inch biscuit cutter into the reserved flour and cut out the biscuits, starting at the outside edge and cutting very close together, being careful not to twist the cutter.

Using a metal spatula if necessary, move the biscuits to the pan or baking sheet. Bake the biscuits on the top rack of the oven for a total of 10 to 14 minutes, depending on thickness, until light golden brown. After 6 minutes, rotate the pan in the oven so that the front of the pan is now turned to the back, and check to see if the bottoms are browning too quickly. If so, slide another baking pan underneath to add insulation and retard browning. Continue baking another 4 to 8 minutes until the biscuits are light golden brown. When the biscuits are done, remove from the oven and lightly brush the tops with softened or melted butter. Turn the biscuits out upside down on a plate to cool slightly. Serve hot, right side up.

Big Nasty Biscuits

Makes 10 to 12 (3-inch) biscuits

Hominy Grill, a James Beard Award–winning Charleston restaurant, is known worldwide for its Southern cooking—including its biscuits. The chef uses cake flour, sugar, and three different fats, giving the biscuits an incredible rich flavor and texture. The restaurant makes a much bigger batch than the average person does, so we've adjusted this recipe. If you want to make them exactly the way Hominy Grill does, use half cake flour and half all-purpose flour plus leaveners as in the directions for making self-rising flour. We found the ratio of cake flour to all-purpose flour to be the same as in self-rising flour, and we have used self-rising flour in this recipe to make it easier for the home cook.

2¼ cups commercial or homemade self-rising flour (page 17), divided

2 teaspoons granulated sugar

2 tablespoons chilled shortening, roughly cut into ¼-inch pieces

1 tablespoon chilled lard

2 tablespoons chilled butter, roughly cut into ¼-inch pieces

1¼ cups milk, divided

Softened butter, for brushing

Preheat oven to 425 degrees F.

Select the baking pan by determining if a soft or crisp exterior is desired. For a soft exterior, use an 8- or 9-inch cake pan, pizza pan, or ovenproof skillet where the biscuits will nestle together snugly, creating the soft exterior while baking. For a crisp exterior, select a baking sheet or other baking pan where the biscuits can be placed wider apart, allowing air to circulate and creating a crisper exterior, and brush the pan with butter.

Fork-sift or whisk 2 cups of the flour and sugar in a large bowl, preferably wider than it is deep, and set aside the remaining ¼ cup. Scatter the pieces of chilled shortening and lard over the flour and work in by rubbing fingers with the fats and flour as if snapping thumb and fingers together (or use two forks or knives, or a pastry cutter) until the mixture looks like oatmeal. After the fats are combined, then evenly toss the butter in and cut using the same snapping method until large flakes of butter transform into what looks like pieces of crumbled feta cheese. Shake the bowl occasionally to allow the larger pieces of fat to bounce to the top of the flour, revealing the largest lumps that still need rubbing. If this method took longer than 5 minutes, place the bowl in the refrigerator for 5 minutes to rechill the fat.

Make a deep hollow in the center of the flour with the back of your hand. Pour 1 cup of milk into the hollow, reserving the remaining ¼ cup, and stir with a rubber spatula or large metal spoon, using broad circular strokes to quickly pull the flour into the milk. Mix just until the dry ingredients are moistened and the sticky dough begins to pull away from the sides of the bowl. If there is some flour remaining in the bottom and sides of the bowl, stir in 1 to 4 tablespoons of reserved milk, just enough to incorporate the remaining flour into the shaggy wettish dough. If the dough is too wet, use more flour when shaping.

Lightly sprinkle a board or other clean surface using some of the reserved flour. Turn the dough out onto the board and sprinkle the top lightly with flour. With floured hands, fold the dough in half, and pat dough out into a ⅓- to ½-inch-thick round, using a little additional flour only if needed. Flour again if necessary, and fold the dough in half a second time. If the dough is still clumpy, pat and fold a third time. Pat dough out into a 1-inch-thick round. Brush off any visible flour from the top. For each biscuit, dip a 3-inch biscuit cutter into the reserved flour and cut out the biscuits,

starting at the outside edge and cutting very close together, being careful not to twist the cutter. The scraps may be combined to make additional biscuits, although these scraps make tougher biscuits. For hand-shaping and other variations, see pages 24–26.

Using a metal spatula if necessary, move the biscuits to the pan or baking sheet. Bake the biscuits on the top rack of the oven for a total of 15 to 20 minutes until light golden brown. After 8 minutes, rotate the pan in the oven so that the front of the pan is now turned to the back, and check to see if the bottoms are browning too quickly. If so, slide another baking pan underneath to add insulation and retard browning. Continue baking another 7 to 12 minutes until the biscuits are light golden brown. When the biscuits are done, remove from the oven and lightly brush the tops with softened or melted butter. Turn the biscuits out upside down on a plate to cool slightly. Serve hot, right side up.

The Flying Biscuit

Makes 18 to 20 (2½-inch) biscuits

The Flying Biscuit Cafe is reputed to have the best biscuit in Atlanta. They churn them out day after day, and moans of pleasure can be heard out on the street by the lines of young and old waiting for a seat. This is supposed to be their recipe—and if it isn't, well, it doesn't matter as this recipe will have people lining up outside any door where these biscuits are being cooked. I mean, how bad could sugar, butter, heavy cream, and half-and-half be?

3¼ cups all-purpose flour, divided

1 tablespoon plus 1½ teaspoons baking powder

½ teaspoon salt

4 tablespoons granulated sugar, divided

¾ cup chilled butter, roughly cut into ½-inch pieces

1 cup heavy cream, divided

⅔ cup half-and-half

1 tablespoon heavy cream, for brushing

Softened butter, for brushing

Preheat oven to 350 degrees F.

Select the baking pan by determining if a soft or crisp exterior is desired. For a soft exterior, use an 8- or 9-inch cake pan, pizza pan, or ovenproof skillet where the biscuits will nestle together snugly, creating the soft exterior while baking. For a crisp exterior, select a baking sheet or other baking pan where the biscuits can be placed wider apart, allowing air to circulate and creating a crisper exterior, and brush the pan with butter.

Fork-sift or whisk 3 cups of flour, baking powder, salt, and 3 tablespoons of sugar in a large bowl, preferably wider than it is deep, and set aside the remaining ¼ cup of flour. Scatter the pieces of chilled butter over the flour and work in by rubbing fingers with the butter and flour as if snapping thumb and fingers together (or use two forks or knives, or a pastry cutter) until the mixture looks like well-crumbled feta cheese, with no piece larger than a pea. Shake the bowl occasionally to allow the larger pieces of fat to bounce to the top of the flour, revealing the largest lumps that still need rubbing. If this method took longer than 5 minutes, place the bowl in the refrigerator for 5 minutes to rechill the fat.

Make a deep hollow in the center of the flour with the back of your hand. Mix ⅔ cup of heavy cream with the half-and-half, reserving the remaining heavy cream. Pour the cream mixture into the hollow and stir with a rubber spatula or large metal spoon, using broad circular strokes to quickly pull the flour into the liquid. Mix just until the dry ingredients are moistened and the sticky dough begins to pull away from the sides of the bowl. If there is some flour remaining on the bottom and sides of the bowl, stir in 1 to 4 tablespoons of reserved cream, just enough to incorporate the remaining flour into the shaggy wettish dough. If the dough is too wet, use more flour when shaping.

Lightly sprinkle a board or other clean surface using some of the reserved flour. Turn the dough out onto the board and sprinkle the top lightly with flour. With floured hands, fold the dough in half, and pat dough out into a ⅓- to ½-inch-thick round, using a little additional flour only if needed. Flour again if necessary, and fold the dough in half a second time. If the dough is still clumpy, pat and fold a third time. Pat dough out into a ½-inch-thick round for a normal biscuit, ¾-inch-thick for a tall biscuit, and 1-inch-thick for a giant biscuit. Brush off any visible flour from the top. For each biscuit, dip a 2½-inch biscuit cutter into the reserved flour and cut out the biscuits, starting at the outside edge and cutting very close together, being careful not to twist the cutter. The scraps may be combined to make additional biscuits, although these scraps make tougher biscuits. For hand-shaping and other variations, see pages 24–26.

Using a metal spatula if necessary, move the biscuits to the pan or baking sheet. Brush the biscuits with 1 tablespoon of the remaining cream and sprinkle with the remaining tablespoon of sugar. Bake the biscuits on the top rack of the oven for a total of 20 minutes, or until light golden brown. After 10 minutes, rotate the pan in the oven so that the front of the pan is now turned to the back, and check to see if the bottoms are browning too quickly. If so, slide another baking pan underneath to add insulation and retard browning. Continue baking another 10 minutes until the biscuits are light golden brown. When the biscuits are done, remove from the oven and lightly brush the tops with softened or melted butter. Turn the biscuits out upside down on a plate to cool slightly. Serve hot, right side up.

Beaten Biscuits

Makes 50 (1¼-inch) biscuits

Initially, these biscuits (sometimes called "ham biscuits") were designed to be stored for a long time, like hardtack. They were beaten 1001 times with wooden boards, rolling pins, or bats. The goal was an absolutely smooth dough that blistered and snapped as it was beaten. Beaten biscuit machines were developed, usually wooden stands holding rollers similar to wringer washers, and a hand crank. A special cutter with "stickers" punched in the tops of the biscuits.

In 1985, I devised the food processor method of "beating" biscuits. The first time I tried it, I burned out my food processor. I learned to avoid very firm doughs. If the machine slows down, turn it off and feel the base to be sure it is still cool. It is better to make two or three smaller batches than to double the quantity of flour unless a large machine is available.

3¼ cups all-purpose flour, divided

1 teaspoon salt

1 teaspoon granulated sugar

1 teaspoon baking powder

1 cup chilled shortening, roughly cut into ½-inch pieces

¾ cup milk, divided

Preheat oven to 350 degrees F.

Pulse together 3 cups of the flour, salt, sugar, and baking powder in a food processor fitted with the knife or dough blade. Set aside the remaining ¼ cup of flour. Scatter the chilled shortening pieces over the flour mixture and pulse until mixture resembles crumbled feta cheese, with no piece larger than a pea. Add ½ cup milk and pulse briefly to incorporate into a shaggy dough. If it is dry or crumbly, add more milk.

If it is too wet, add more flour. "Knead" in the food processor a few minutes until it is smooth, removing it if the food processor starts to whine or stagger on the board, then turn out onto a floured board. Sometimes all the beating can be done in the food processor. When it's ready, the dough should "snap" when you hit it and feel very smooth. If it is not, beat the dough briefly on the counter with a rolling pin until it "snaps"—how long depends on the dough when it comes out of the processor. Fold the dough in half to make the biscuits easier to split later.

Add more liquid if flour is too dry.

Starting from the outside of the dough and working toward the center, avoiding the fold, cut small rounds with a 1¼-inch biscuit cutter. Combine the scraps, fold over, and roll if

BEATEN BISCUITS

This is the most laborious of cakes, and also the most unwholesome . . . We do not recommend it; but there is no accounting for tastes. Children should not eat these biscuits—nor grown persons either, if they can get any other sort of bread. When living in a town where there are bakers, there is no excuse for making Maryland (beaten) biscuits . . . Better to live on Indian cakes.

—Directions for Cookery in its Various Branches,
Eliza Leslie, 1837

necessary. Cut out the rest of the dough, rolling and folding scraps as necessary. Press a fork down in the top of each round, followed by a parallel set of holes.

Move the biscuits to a lightly greased baking sheet. Bake for 30 minutes until crisp and, preferably, still white or only lightly dappled with brown. They should open easily when split with a fork. They will keep for weeks tightly covered in a tin or in the freezer. Split in two before serving.

GEORGIA BEATEN BISCUIT

1 teaspoon salt

1 quart pastry flour

6 tablespoons lard

1 cup sweet milk, ice cold, more or less, to make a stiff dough

Sift salt into the flour, mix in the lard, add the sweet milk, being very careful to have the dough very stiff, even if you leave out some of the milk. Beat or grind in biscuit break for 20 minutes. Cut ½-inch thick with a small cutter made for beaten biscuits with stickers in center (or stick with a fork), bake in slow oven 20 to 40 minutes, until brown and crisp.

—Southern Cooking,
Mrs. S. R. Dull, 1928

Make-Ahead Shenandoah Valley Biscuits

Makes 10 (2½-inch) biscuits

I had always been told biscuits could not be made in advance. When Cynthia and I trekked to New York for my appearance on Good Morning America, *we took unbaked biscuits. We froze them in a freezer there as we were unsure about prep space and time. We baked the biscuits there the next morning at some ungodly hour and were thrilled to find they were perfectly fine. This recipe from the Shenandoah Valley recommends resting the biscuits on a baking sheet (or cake pan, etc.) in the refrigerator for 2 hours or overnight. Resting allows the fat to chill, the baking powder to act, and produces a higher-rising biscuit. This is true of many biscuits.*

2¼ cups all-purpose flour, divided

1 teaspoon baking powder

½ teaspoon salt

¼ cup chilled butter, roughly cut into ¼-inch pieces
AND
¼ cup chilled butter, roughly cut into ½-inch pieces

⅔ cup milk, divided

Preheat oven to 400 degrees F.

Select the baking pan by determining if a soft or crisp exterior is desired. For a soft exterior, use an 8- or 9-inch cake pan, pizza pan, or ovenproof skillet where the biscuits will nestle together snugly, creating the soft exterior while baking. For a crisp exterior, select a baking sheet or other baking pan where the biscuits can be placed wider apart, allowing air to circulate and creating a crisper exterior, and brush the pan with butter.

Fork-sift or whisk 2 cups of flour, baking powder, and salt in a large bowl, preferably wider than it is deep, and set aside the remaining ¼ cup of flour. Scatter the ¼-inch-size pieces of chilled butter over the flour and work in by rubbing fingers with the fat and flour as if snapping thumb and fingers together (or use two forks or knives, or a pastry cutter) until the mixture looks like well-crumbled feta cheese. Scatter the ½-inch-size pieces of chilled butter over the flour mixture and continue snapping thumb and fingers together until no pieces remain larger than a pea. Shake the bowl occasionally to allow the larger pieces of fat to bounce to the top of the flour, revealing the largest lumps that still need rubbing. If this method took longer than 5 minutes, place the bowl in the refrigerator for 5 minutes to rechill the fat.

Make a deep hollow in the center of the flour with the back of your hand. Pour ⅓ cup of the milk into the hollow, reserving ⅓ cup milk, and stir with a rubber spatula or large metal spoon, using broad circular strokes to quickly pull the flour into the milk. Mix just until the dry ingredients are moistened and the sticky dough begins to pull away from the sides of the bowl. If there is some flour remaining on the bottom and sides of the bowl, stir in 1 to 4 tablespoons of reserved milk, just enough to incorporate the remaining flour into the shaggy wettish dough. If the dough is too wet, use more flour when shaping.

Lightly sprinkle a board or other clean surface using some of the reserved flour. Turn the dough out onto the board and sprinkle the top lightly with flour. With floured hands, fold the dough in half, and pat dough out into a ⅓- to ½-inch-thick round, using a little additional flour only if needed. Flour again if necessary, and fold the dough in half a second time. If the dough is still clumpy, pat and fold a third time. Pat dough out into a ½-inch-thick round for a normal biscuit, ¾-inch-thick for a tall biscuit, and 1-inch-thick for a giant biscuit. Brush off any visible flour from the top. For each biscuit,

dip a 2½-inch biscuit cutter into the reserved flour and cut out the biscuits, starting at the outside edge and cutting very close together, being careful not to twist the cutter. The scraps may be combined to make additional biscuits, although these scraps make tougher biscuits. For hand-shaping and other variations, see pages 24–26.

Using a metal spatula if necessary, move the biscuits to the pan or baking sheet and cover with plastic wrap. Refrigerate two hours or overnight, or freeze. Preheat the oven to 450 degrees F and bake the still-cold or frozen biscuits on the top rack of the oven for a total of 10 to 14 minutes until light golden brown. After 6 minutes, rotate the pan in the oven so that the front of the pan is now turned to the back, and check to see if the bottoms are browning too quickly. If so, slide another baking pan underneath to add insulation and retard browning. Continue baking another 4 to 8 minutes until the biscuits are light golden brown. When the biscuits are done, remove from the oven and lightly brush the tops with softened or melted butter. Turn the biscuits out upside down on a plate to cool slightly. Serve hot, right side up.

Mrs. Dull's Humble Soda Biscuits

Makes 12 (2-inch) biscuits

Mrs. Dull is my guru. I always check her cookbook, Southern Cooking, *whenever I'm in doubt! She wrote her book during hard times— during wars, depressions, and other such times— thus her use of only ¼ cup of shortening. She prefers a ½ teaspoon of soda for each cup of tart buttermilk. She specifically states that day-old buttermilk, leaning towards souring, is preferable. Amazingly, the biscuits are as light, fluffy, and flavorful as those with twice as much fat.*

2¼ cups all-purpose flour, divided

1 teaspoon salt

½ teaspoon baking soda

2 tablespoons chilled shortening, roughly cut into ¼-inch pieces
AND
2 tablespoons chilled shortening, roughly cut into ½-inch pieces

1¼ cup buttermilk, divided

Melted butter for serving, if desired

Preheat oven to 350 degrees F.

Select the baking pan by determining if a soft or crisp exterior is desired. For a soft exterior, use an 8- or 9-inch cake pan, pizza pan, or ovenproof skillet where the biscuits will nestle together snugly, creating the soft exterior while baking. For a crisp exterior, select a baking sheet or other baking pan where the biscuits can be placed wider apart, allowing air to circulate and creating a crisper exterior, and brush the pan with butter.

Fork-sift or whisk 2 cups of the flour, salt, and baking soda in a large bowl, preferably wider than it is deep, and set aside the remaining ¼ cup of flour. Scatter the ¼-inch-size pieces of chilled shortening over the flour and work in by rubbing fingers with the fat and flour as if snapping thumb and fingers together (or use two forks or knives, or a pastry cutter) until the mixture looks like well-crumbled feta cheese. Scatter the ½-inch-size pieces of chilled shortening over the flour mixture and continue snapping thumb and fingers together until no pieces remain larger than a pea. Shake the bowl occasionally to allow the larger pieces of fat to bounce to the top of the flour, revealing the largest lumps that still need rubbing. If this method took longer than 5 minutes, place the bowl in the refrigerator for 5 minutes to rechill the fat.

Make a deep hollow in the center of the flour with the back of your hand. Pour 1 cup of buttermilk into the hollow, reserving the remaining ¼ cup, and stir with a rubber spatula or large metal spoon, using broad circular strokes to quickly pull the flour into the buttermilk. Mix just until the dry ingredients are moistened and the sticky dough begins to pull away from the sides of the bowl. If there is some flour remaining in the bottom and sides of the bowl, stir in 1 to 4 tablespoons of reserved buttermilk, just enough to incorporate the remaining flour into the shaggy wettish dough. If the dough is too wet, use more flour when shaping.

Lightly sprinkle a board or other clean surface using some of the reserved flour. Turn the dough out onto the board and sprinkle the top lightly with flour. With floured hands, fold the dough in half, and pat dough out into a ⅓- to ½-inch-thick round, using a little additional flour only if needed. Flour again if necessary, and fold the dough in half a second time. If the dough is still clumpy, pat and fold a third time. Pat dough out into a ½-inch-thick round for a normal biscuit, ¾-inch-thick for a tall biscuit, and 1-inch-thick for a giant biscuit. Brush off any visible flour from the top. For each biscuit, dip a 2-inch biscuit cutter into the reserved flour and cut out the biscuits, starting at the outside edge and cutting very close together, being careful not to twist the cutter. The scraps may be combined to make additional biscuits, although these scraps make tougher biscuits. For hand-shaping and other variations, see pages 24–26.

Using a metal spatula if necessary, move the biscuits to the pan or baking sheet. Bake the biscuits on the top rack of the oven for a total of 10 to 14 minutes until

TYPES OF FLOUR

"To test for pastry flour, also known as soft-wheat flour and cake flour, squeeze tight a handful of flour. If it clings together and shows each fingerprint and wrinkle, it is a pastry flour. It should also feel smooth and starchy to the touch. Bread flour when rolled between the fingers and thumb, and will feel grainy when squeezed in the hand, will fall apart instead of staying tightly packed."

—*Southern Cooking,*
Mrs. S. R. Dull, 1928

When Nathalie saw pasta made in Italy, the tester did the same test with the incoming flour to make sure it performed correctly.

light golden brown. After 6 minutes, rotate the pan in the oven so that the front of the pan is now turned to the back, and check to see if the bottoms are browning too quickly. If so, slide another baking pan underneath to add insulation and retard browning. Continue baking another 4 to 8 minutes, until the biscuits are light golden brown. When the biscuits are done, remove from the oven and lightly brush the tops with softened or melted butter. Turn the biscuits out upside down on a plate to cool slightly. Serve hot, right side up.

Gullah Biscuits

Makes 12 (2½-inch) biscuits

The summer heat of the barrier islands off South Carolina and Georgia can take your breath away, and one can only imagine how hot it is in the kitchen. We doubt that even shortening could stand up to the summer heat and therefore might explain the use of salad oil in these biscuits from Sallie Ann Robinson in Gullah Home Cooking the Daufuskie Way. *The eggs help provide a very high rise.*

2¼ cups all-purpose flour, divided

3 teaspoons baking powder

1 teaspoon salt

5 teaspoons vegetable oil

2 large eggs

1¼ cups milk or buttermilk, divided

Softened butter, for brushing

Preheat oven to 350 degrees F.

Select the baking pan by determining if a soft or crisp exterior is desired. For a soft exterior, use an 8- or 9-inch cake pan, pizza pan, or ovenproof skillet where the biscuits will nestle together snugly, creating the soft exterior while baking. For a crisp exterior, select a baking sheet or other baking pan where the biscuits can be placed wider apart, allowing air to circulate and creating a crisper exterior, and brush the pan with butter.

Fork-sift or whisk 2 cups of the flour, baking powder, and salt in a large bowl, preferably wider than it is deep, and set aside the remaining ¼ cup of flour. Fold in the cooking oil.

Make a deep hollow in the center of the flour with the back of your hand. Lightly beat the eggs with 1 cup of the buttermilk, reserving the remaining ¼ cup, and pour into the hollow. Stir with a rubber spatula or large metal spoon, using broad circular strokes to quickly pull the flour into the liquid. Mix just until the dry ingredients are moistened and the sticky dough begins to pull away from the sides of the bowl. If there is some flour remaining on the bottom and sides of the bowl, stir in 1 to 4 tablespoons of reserved buttermilk, just enough to incorporate the remaining flour into the shaggy wettish dough. If the dough is too wet, use more flour when shaping.

Lightly sprinkle a board or other clean surface using some of the reserved flour. Turn the dough out onto the board and sprinkle the top lightly with flour. With floured hands, fold the dough in half, and pat dough out into a ⅓- to ½-inch-thick round, using a little additional flour only if needed. Flour again if necessary, and fold the dough in half a second time. If the dough is still clumpy, pat and fold a third time. Pat dough out into a ½-inch-thick round for a normal biscuit, ¾-inch-thick for a tall biscuit, and 1-inch-thick for a giant biscuit. Brush off any visible flour from the top. For each biscuit, dip a 2½-inch biscuit cutter into the reserved flour and cut out the biscuits, starting at the outside edge and cutting very close together, being careful not to twist the cutter. The scraps may be combined to make additional biscuits, although these scraps make tougher biscuits. For hand-shaping and other variations, see pages 24–26.

Using a metal spatula if necessary, move the biscuits to the pan or baking sheet. Bake the biscuits on the top rack of the oven for a total of 20 to 25 minutes, depending on thickness, until light golden brown. After 10 minutes, rotate the pan in the oven so that the front of the pan is now turned to the back, and check to see if the bottoms are browning too quickly. If so, slide another baking pan underneath to add insulation and retard browning. Continue baking another 10 to 15 minutes until the biscuits are light golden brown. When the biscuits are done, remove from the oven and lightly brush the tops with softened or melted butter. Turn the biscuits out upside down on a plate to cool slightly. Serve hot, right side up.

Olive Oil Biscuits

Makes 12 biscuits

Just after reading what we thought was a crazy recipe for biscuits used as pizza crust, we stumbled upon an olive oil biscuit recipe. Well, it was almost as if the biscuit gods looked us right in the eyes and said, "Don't doubt the versatility of the biscuit!" As soon as these savory olive oil biscuits came out of the oven, we said, "Wow, I would definitely use this recipe as either a biscuit or a pizza dough." The subtle flavor of rich olives permeates the flakes of biscuit and would pair nicely with any soup or even with a sliced tomato tucked in between its halves.

2¼ cups commercial or homemade self-rising flour (page 17), divided

2 tablespoons olive oil

1 cup buttermilk, divided

Softened butter, for brushing

Preheat oven to 425 degrees F.

Select the baking pan by determining if a soft or crisp exterior is desired. For a soft exterior, use an 8- or 9-inch cake pan, pizza pan, or ovenproof skillet where the biscuits will nestle together snugly, creating the soft exterior while baking. For a crisp exterior, select a baking sheet or other baking pan where the biscuits can be placed wider apart, allowing air to circulate and creating a crisper exterior, and brush the pan with butter.

Fork-sift or whisk 2 cups of the flour in a large bowl, preferably wider than it is deep, and set aside the remaining ¼ cup of flour. Make a deep hollow in the center of the flour with the back of your hand. Pour the oil into ¾ cup of the buttermilk, reserving ¼ cup buttermilk, and then pour the combined liquids into the hollow. Stir with a rubber spatula or large metal spoon, using broad circular strokes to quickly pull the flour into the liquid. Mix just until the dry ingredients are moistened and the sticky dough begins to pull away from the sides of the bowl. If there is some flour remaining on the bottom and sides of the bowl, stir in 1 to 4 tablespoons of reserved buttermilk, just enough to incorporate the remaining flour into the shaggy wettish dough. If the dough is too wet, use more flour when shaping.

Lightly sprinkle a board or other clean surface using some of the reserved flour. Turn the dough out onto the board and sprinkle the top lightly with flour. With floured hands, fold the dough in half, and pat dough out into a 1/3- to 1/2-inch-thick round, using a little additional flour only if needed. Flour again if necessary, and fold the dough in half a second time. If the dough is still clumpy, pat and fold a third time. Pat dough out into a 1/2-inch-thick round for a normal biscuit, 3/4-inch-thick for a tall biscuit, and 1-inch-thick for a giant biscuit. Brush off any visible flour from the top. For each biscuit, dip a 2 1/2-inch biscuit cutter into the reserved flour and cut out the biscuits, starting at the outside edge and cutting very close together, being careful not to twist the cutter. The scraps may be combined to make additional biscuits, although these scraps make tougher biscuits. For hand-shaping and other variations, see pages 24–26.

Using a metal spatula if necessary, move the biscuits to the pan or baking sheet. Bake the biscuits on the top rack of the oven for a total of 10 to 14 minutes, depending on thickness, until light golden brown. After 6 minutes, rotate the pan in the oven so that the front of the pan is now turned to the back, and check to see if the bottoms are browning too quickly. If so, slide another baking pan underneath to add insulation and retard browning. Continue baking another 4 to 8 minutes until the biscuits are light golden brown. When the biscuits are done, remove from the oven and lightly brush the tops with softened or melted butter. Turn the biscuits out upside down on a plate to cool slightly. Serve hot, right side up.

VARIATION: For a pizza biscuit dough, pat out to 1/4 inches thick on a 12-inch pizza pan. Top as with any uncooked pizza dough. Bake at 350 to 400 degrees F for 18 to 20 minutes.

Buttermilk-Margarine Biscuits

Makes 12 (2½-inch) biscuits

A friend whose family always used margarine gave us this recipe.

2¼ cups all-purpose flour, divided

1 tablespoon baking powder

½ teaspoon salt

¼ cup chilled margarine, roughly cut into ½-inch pieces

1¼ cups buttermilk, divided

Softened margarine, for brushing

Preheat oven to 375 degrees F.

Select the baking pan by determining if a soft or crisp exterior is desired. For a soft exterior, use an 8- or 9-inch cake pan, pizza pan, or ovenproof skillet where the biscuits will nestle together snugly, creating the soft exterior while baking. For a crisp exterior, select a baking sheet or other baking pan where the biscuits can be placed wider apart, allowing air to circulate and creating a crisper exterior, and brush the pan with butter.

Fork-sift or whisk 2 cups of the flour, baking powder, and salt in a large bowl, preferably wider than it is deep, and set aside the remaining ¼ cup of flour. Scatter the pieces of chilled margarine over the flour and work in by rubbing fingers with the margarine and flour as if snapping thumb and fingers together (or use two forks or knives, or a pastry cutter) until the mixture looks like well-crumbled feta cheese, with no piece larger than a pea. Shake the bowl occasionally to allow the larger pieces of fat to bounce to the top of the flour, revealing the largest lumps that still need rubbing. If this method took longer than 5 minutes, refrigerate for 5 minutes to rechill the fat.

Make a deep hollow in the center of the flour with the back of your hand. Pour 1 cup of buttermilk into the hollow, reserving the remaining ¼ cup, and stir with a rubber spatula or large metal spoon, using broad circular strokes to quickly pull the flour into the liquid. Mix just until the dry ingredients are moistened and the sticky dough begins to pull away from the sides of the bowl. If there is some flour remaining on the bottom and sides of the bowl, stir in 1 to 4 tablespoons of reserved buttermilk, just enough to incorporate the remaining flour into the shaggy wettish dough. If the dough is too wet, use more flour when shaping.

Lightly sprinkle a board or other clean surface using some of the reserved flour. Turn the dough out onto the board and sprinkle the top lightly with flour. With floured hands, fold the dough in half, and pat dough out into a ⅓- to ½-inch-thick round, using a little additional flour only if needed. Flour again if necessary, and fold the dough in half a second time. If the dough is still clumpy, pat and fold a third time. Pat dough out into a ½-inch-thick round for a normal biscuit, ¾-inch-thick for a tall biscuit, and 1-inch-thick for a giant biscuit. Brush off any visible flour from the top. For each biscuit, dip a 2½-inch biscuit cutter into the reserved flour and cut out the biscuits, starting at the outside edge and cutting very close together, being

careful not to twist the cutter. The scraps may be combined to make additional biscuits, although these scraps make tougher biscuits. For hand-shaping and other variations, see pages 24–26.

Using a metal spatula if necessary, move the biscuits to the pan or baking sheet. Bake the biscuits on the top rack of the oven for a total of 14 to 17 minutes, depending on thickness, until light golden brown. After 7 minutes, rotate the pan in the oven so that the front of the pan is now turned to the back, and check to see if the bottoms are browning too quickly. If so, slide another baking pan underneath to add insulation and retard browning. Continue baking another 7 to 10 minutes until the biscuits are light golden brown. When the biscuits are done, remove from the oven and lightly brush the tops with softened or melted margarine. Turn the biscuits out upside down on a plate to cool slightly. Serve hot, right side up.

Angel Biscuits

Makes 30 to 40 (2-inch) Biscuits

Angel Biscuits (also known as Bride's Biscuits because they are foolproof) are a Southern combination of biscuit and yeast roll. The technique of folding over the dough allows the biscuits to split easily for generous buttering and appears a bit to be like angel's wings, hence the name. Since the dough can be refrigerated for a week, the biscuits can be baked over a period of days, which is particularly useful for today's small families. They freeze well, and no one would guess if the whole batch was baked and frozen, tightly wrapped, and then defrosted for use.

1 package active dry yeast

¼ cup granulated sugar

3 tablespoons warm water (110–115 degrees F)

5–6 cups commercial or homemade
self-rising flour (page 17)

1 teaspoon baking soda

½ teaspoon salt

½ cup shortening, room temperature

½ cup butter, room temperature

2 cups buttermilk, room temperature

Melted butter, for finishing

Dissolve the yeast and sugar in the warm water in a small bowl and set aside.

Fork-sift or whisk 5 cups of the self-rising flour, baking soda, and salt in a large bowl, preferably wider than it is deep. Break the shortening and butter into pieces and scatter over the flour. Work in by rubbing fingers with the fat and flour as if snapping thumb and fingers together (or use two forks or knives, or a pastry cutter) until the mixture looks like well-crumbled feta cheese.

Make a deep hollow in the center of the flour with the back of one hand. Stir the yeast mixture into the buttermilk and pour this mixture into the hollow, stirring with a long wooden spoon. Add flour as needed to make a very damp, shaggy dough.

Flour a clean working surface and turn the dough out onto the flour. With floured hands, knead the dough by folding in half, pushing out, refolding, and turning the dough clockwise until the dough is tender (like a baby's bottom), about 10 minutes by hand. Add flour as necessary to make a supple dough. There are three options at this point: 1) shape now, 2) for an even lighter biscuit, move to an oiled plastic bag and let rise until doubled, then punch down and proceed to shape, or 3) refrigerate up to one week and use as desired.

When ready to use, divide dough in half to shape easily. Roll dough out into a ⅓- to ½-inch-thick round. Fold in half and roll or pat out again until ⅔ to 1 inch thick. Repeat with second half as desired.

For each biscuit, dip a 2-inch biscuit cutter into the reserved flour and cut out the biscuits, starting at the outside edge and cutting very close together, being careful not to twist the cutter. Move the biscuits to a greased baking sheet. Let double at room temperature, about 30 minutes.

Preheat oven to 400 degrees F. Bake the biscuits on the middle rack of the oven. After 6 minutes, rotate the pan in the oven so that the front of the pan is now turned to the back; check to see if the bottoms are burning too quickly. If so, slide another baking sheet underneath to add insulation and retard browning. Continue baking another 6 to 9 minutes as needed, until a light golden brown. When the biscuits are done, remove from the oven and lightly brush the tops with softened or melted butter. Turn the biscuits out upside down on a plate to cool slightly. (If an angel-like touch is desired, sprinkle with flour.) Serve hot, right side up.

ANGEL WINGS

To make angel wings, cut folded biscuits into 2½-inch circles. Cut in half, brush with milk along the curved side of both halves, move to a greased baking sheet with the two curved, moistened sides touching and bake as directed in the recipe.

Prepare to fold the dough.

Stir 'n Roll Biscuits

Makes 12 (2½-inch) biscuits

Adapted from the 1974 edition of Betty Crocker's Cookbook, *these were a typical biscuit when I was growing up. Although they aren't my favorite, they will do in a pinch.*

2 cups all-purpose flour

1 tablespoon baking powder

1 teaspoon salt

⅓ cup salad oil

⅔ cup milk

Preheat oven to 425 degrees F.

Combine flour, baking powder, and salt. Pour oil and milk all at once into the flour mixture. Turn onto waxed paper, fold the dough over by lifting one corner of the paper to fold it. Pull paper back and repeat until the dough looks smooth. Pat or roll ½ inch thick between 2 sheets of waxed paper. Cut dough with unfloured biscuit cutter. Place biscuits on ungreased baking sheet and bake 10 to 12 minutes until golden brown.

Leftover Biscuits

BISCUIT TOAST

Serves 1

No biscuit should ever go to waste, not even the stalest. This revives the biscuit, creating a Southern comfort food, beloved by children and grown-ups alike. The initial water softens the biscuit slightly before it is quickly dumped off. The milk soaks in and flavors the biscuit.

1 biscuit, halved

1 cup boiling water

1 cup very hot milk

1 tablespoon butter, softened

Freshly ground black pepper

Cut a biscuit in half horizontally. Toast the cut side of each half and move to a shallow bowl. Pour the boiling water over the biscuit and then quickly pour it off. Add the hot milk and butter, and season to taste with pepper (it shouldn't need salt). Serve immediately.

PAN-FRIED BISCUITS

Serves 1

Now that my friend Kate Almand's husband, David, has passed on, she makes up a batch of biscuits early in the week and then reheats them this way every day for breakfast.

1 biscuit

1 tablespoon butter

Split the biscuit in half horizontally. Heat the butter in a heavy frying pan. When starting to brown, add the biscuit sides, split side down. Cook until brown. Remove and eat hot.

BROWNED BISCUITS

Serves 1

Toasted biscuits fill the bill for a hot breakfast and, of course, mask the obvious—they are leftovers.

1 biscuit

Split the biscuit horizontally. Move to a hot oven and toast until cut side is brown. Eat hot with plenty of butter.

Savory Sweet Potato
Biscuits with Ham

Embellished Biscuits

Biscuits can be dressed up with just a little of this and that to make a splash at a party or just a little different variation to surprise the family. Embellish a plain biscuit with a little dried fruit or lots of black pepper, and there is still that response of "Yum, these are so good!" to greet the baker.

A change of ingredients—goat butter is one of my favorites—and a totally different biscuit is produced. My friend Barbara Morgan's Half-Dollar Ham Biscuits (page 126) have been a favorite of mine for many years. She makes them ahead and refrigerates or freezes them, and they are ready to go for a bridge lunch or a grand party.

Senator Holling's Flaky Appetizer Cream Cheese Biscuits (page 130) melt in the mouth, alone or with anything from Hot Pepper Jelly (page 176) to the best Easy Refrigerator Strawberry Jam (page 174).

Once biscuits are mastered, this step up to glory is an easy one.

Black Pepper Biscuits

Makes 16 to 18 (2-inch) biscuits

Almost any cracked or ground spice is happy in a biscuit dough. This bakes up as a special treat, particularly to sandwich ham or chicken or to top a casserole or soup.

2¼ cups all-purpose flour, divided

1 tablespoon baking powder

½ teaspoon salt

½ to 1 tablespoon freshly ground black pepper

½ teaspoon baking soda

¼ cup chilled shortening, roughly cut into ¼-inch pieces
AND
¼ cup chilled shortening, roughly cut into ½-inch pieces

1 cup buttermilk, divided

Softened butter, for brushing

Preheat oven to 450 degrees F.

Select the baking pan by determining if a soft or crisp exterior is desired. For a soft exterior, use an 8- or 9-inch cake pan, pizza pan, or ovenproof skillet where the biscuits will nestle together snugly, creating the soft exterior while baking. For a crisp exterior, select a baking sheet or other baking pan where the biscuits can be placed wider apart, allowing air to circulate and creating a crisper exterior, and brush the pan with butter.

Fork-sift or whisk 2 cups of flour, baking powder, salt, pepper, and baking soda in a large bowl, preferably wider than it is deep, and set aside the remaining ¼ cup of flour. Scatter the ¼-inch-size pieces of chilled fat over the flour and work in by rubbing fingers with the fat and flour as if snapping thumb and fingers together (or use two forks or knives, or a pastry cutter) until the mixture looks like well-crumbled feta cheese. Scatter the ½-inch-size pieces of chilled fat over the flour mixture and continue snapping thumb and fingers together until no pieces remain larger than a pea. Shake the bowl occasionally to allow the larger pieces of fat to bounce to the top of the flour, revealing the largest lumps that still need rubbing. If this method took longer than 5 minutes, place the bowl in the refrigerator for 5 minutes to rechill the fat.

Make a deep hollow in the center of the flour with the back of your hand. Pour ¾ cup of buttermilk into the hollow, reserving ¼ cup, and stir with a rubber spatula or large metal spoon, using broad circular strokes to quickly pull the flour into the milk. Mix just until the dry ingredients are moistened and the sticky dough begins to pull away from the sides of the bowl. If there is some flour remaining on the bottom and sides of the bowl, stir in 1 to 4 tablespoons of reserved buttermilk, just enough to incorporate the remaining flour into the shaggy wettish dough. If the dough is too wet, use more flour when shaping.

Lightly sprinkle a board or other clean surface with some of the reserved flour. Turn the dough out onto the board and sprinkle the top lightly with flour. With floured hands, fold the dough in half and pat it into a ⅓- to ½-inch-thick round, using a little additional flour only if needed. Flour again if necessary, and fold the dough in half a second time. If the dough is still clumpy, pat and fold a third time. Pat dough out into a ½-inch-thick round for a normal biscuit, ¾-inch-thick for a tall biscuit, and 1-inch-thick for a giant biscuit. Brush off any visible flour from the top. For each biscuit, dip a 2-inch biscuit cutter into the reserved flour and cut out the biscuits, starting at the outside edge and cutting very close together, being careful not to twist the cutter. The scraps may be combined to make additional biscuits, although these scraps make tougher biscuits. For hand-shaping and other variations, see pages 24–26.

Using a metal spatula if necessary, move the biscuits to the pan or baking sheet. Bake the biscuits on the top rack of the oven for a total of 10 to 14 minutes until light golden brown. After 6 minutes, rotate the pan in the oven so that the front of the pan is now turned to the back, and check to see if the bottoms are browning too quickly. If so, slide another baking pan underneath to add insulation and retard browning. Continue baking another 4 to 8 minutes until the biscuits are light golden brown. When the biscuits are done, remove from the oven and lightly brush the tops with softened or melted butter. Turn the biscuits out upside down on a plate to cool slightly. Serve hot, right side up.

VARIATION: Add 1 tablespoon of ground coriander seed or fennel seed to the dough for biscuits that are both particularly good when sandwiching pork and shrimp.

VARIATION: BACON PEPPER BISCUITS

Add ½ cup cooked and crumbled bacon to the dough before adding the buttermilk.

goat Butter Biscuits

Makes 10 to 12 (2½-inch) biscuits

Wow! That is the only word to describe these
creamy rich biscuits and their remarkable
lingering aftertaste. They are incredibly tangy
but not overwhelmingly so. They not only pack
an intense flavor punch, but they are also some
of the most beautiful biscuits I've ever seen—
burnished on top, little dimples, and a rise that
I thought could have been achieved only with
tons of baking powder. Hayley Daen reached
for the goat milk butter when we were shopping
one day and suggested we try it. We had no idea
they would become one of our favorite biscuits;
but they are. They need nothing more, and
are good hours—even a day or two—later at
room temperature or heated. If goat butter were
available everywhere, it might be the only biscuit
I'd eat.

2¼ cups commercial or homemade
self-rising flour (page 17), divided

¼ cup chilled goat milk butter,
roughly cut into ¼-inch pieces
AND
¼ cup chilled goat milk butter,
roughly cut into ½-inch pieces

1 cup milk, divided

Softened butter, for brushing

Preheat oven to 425 degrees F.

Select the baking pan by determining if a soft or crisp exterior is desired. For a soft exterior, use an 8- or 9-inch cake pan, pizza pan, or ovenproof skillet where the biscuits will nestle together snugly, creating the soft exterior while baking. For a crisp exterior, select a baking sheet or other baking pan where the biscuits can be placed wider apart, allowing air to circulate and creating a crisper exterior, and brush the pan with butter.

Fork-sift or whisk 2 cups of flour in a large bowl, preferably wider than deep, and set aside the remaining ¼ cup. Scatter the ¼-inch-size pieces of chilled goat milk butter over the flour and work in by rubbing fingers with the fat and flour as if snapping thumb and fingers together (or use two forks or knives, or a pastry cutter) until the mixture looks like well-crumbled feta cheese. Scatter the ½-inch-size pieces of chilled goat milk butter over the flour mixture and continue snapping thumb and fingers together until no pieces remain larger than a pea. Shake the bowl occasionally to allow the larger pieces of fat to bounce to the top of the flour, revealing the largest lumps that still need rubbing. If this method took longer than 5 minutes, place the bowl in the refrigerator for 5 minutes to rechill the fat.

Make a deep hollow in the center of the flour with the back of your hand. Pour ¾ cup of the milk into the hollow, reserving ¼ cup, and stir the milk, using broad circular strokes to quickly pull the flour into the milk. Mix just until the dry ingredients are moistened and the sticky dough begins to pull away from the sides of the bowl. If there is some flour remaining on the bottom and sides of the bowl, stir in 1 to 4 tablespoons of reserved milk, just enough to incorporate the remaining flour into the shaggy wettish dough. If the dough is too wet, use more flour when shaping.

Lightly sprinkle a board or other clean surface with some of the reserved flour. Turn the dough out onto the board and sprinkle the top lightly with flour. With floured hands, fold the dough in half, and pat dough out into a ⅓- to ½-inch-thick round, using a little additional flour only if needed. Flour again if necessary, and fold the dough in half a second time. If the dough is still clumpy, pat and fold a third time. Pat dough out into a ½-inch-thick round for a normal biscuit, ¾-inch-thick for a tall biscuit, and 1-inch-thick for a giant biscuit. Brush off any visible flour from the top. For each biscuit, dip a 2-inch biscuit cutter into the reserved flour and cut out the biscuits, starting at the outside edge and cutting very close together, being careful not to twist the cutter. The scraps may be combined to make additional biscuits, although these scraps make tougher biscuits. For hand-shaping and other variations, see pages 24–26.

Using a metal spatula if necessary, move the biscuits to the pan or baking sheet. Bake the biscuits on the top rack of the oven for a total of 10 to 14 minutes until light golden brown. After 6 minutes, rotate the pan in the oven so that the front of the pan is now turned to the back, and check to see if the bottoms are browning too quickly. If so, slide another baking pan underneath to add insulation and retard browning. Continue baking another 4 to 8 minutes until the biscuits are light golden brown. When the biscuits are done, lightly brush the tops with melted butter. Turn the biscuits out upside down on a plate to cool slightly. Serve hot, right side up. To gild the lily, split and fill with goat butter. You might think you've died and gone to heaven.

VARIATION: Use goat milk rather than whole milk, remembering that the thinner the milk, the less is needed.

Measure the thickness of the dough.

105

Pimento Cheese Biscuits

Makes 18 (1-inch) biscuits

"Pimentocheese" is almost one word in the South, along with "ratcheese." Pimento peppers—pointed red peppers similar to a bell pepper—were grown and canned in Georgia through 1970. They were mixed with mayonnaise and "ratcheese," which was a large round of yellow American cheese similar to cheddar cheese. Ratcheese was kept in a round wooden container until ready to see, when it was placed under a glass "bell" and kept on a wooden board. It is found in grocery stores, delis, and even gas stations, and is used as a paste on white bread (fresh or toasted), cucumbers, and many other foods.

2¼ cups commercial or homemade
self-rising flour (page 17), divided

1 cup shredded sharp cheddar cheese

¼ cup chilled butter, roughly
cut into ¼-inch pieces
AND
¼ cup chilled butter, roughly
cut into ½-inch pieces

1 (4-ounce) jar pimento or roasted
red bell peppers, chopped

¼ cup finely chopped onion (optional)

1 cup buttermilk, divided

2 tablespoons melted butter

Softened butter, for brushing

Preheat oven to 450 degrees F.

Pulse 2 cups of flour with the cheese two or three times in a food processor fitted with the knife or dough blade. Set aside ¼ cup of flour. Scatter the ¼-inch shortening pieces over the flour mixture and pulse 2 or 3 times. Scatter the ½-inch shortening pieces over the flour mixture and pulse 2 or 3 times until mixture resembles well-crumbled feta cheese, with no piece larger than a pea. Add the pimentos, onion, and ¾ cup of buttermilk. Set aside the ¼ cup buttermilk. Pulse mixture briefly to incorporate into a shaggy wettish dough. When the blade stops, remove the lid and feel the dough. Add reserved buttermilk or flour as needed to make a slightly wettish dough. Pulse once or twice more until the dough looks shaggy but holds together.

Lightly sprinkle a board or other clean surface with some of the reserved flour. Turn the dough out onto the board and sprinkle the top lightly with flour. With floured hands, fold the dough in half, and pat dough out into a ⅓- to ½-inch-thick round, using a little additional flour only if needed. Flour again if necessary, and fold the dough in half a second time. If the dough is still clumpy, pat and fold a third time. Pat dough out into a ½-inch-thick round for a normal biscuit, ¾-inch-thick for a tall biscuit, and 1-inch-thick for a giant biscuit. Brush off any visible flour from the top. For each biscuit, dip a 2-inch biscuit cutter into the reserved flour and cut out the biscuits, starting at the outside edge and cutting very close together, being careful not to twist the cutter. The scraps may be combined to make additional biscuits, although these scraps make tougher biscuits.

Using a metal spatula if necessary, move the biscuits to a lightly greased baking sheet so they are touching each other. Bake the biscuits on the top rack of the oven for a total of 13 to 15 minutes until light golden brown. After 6 minutes, rotate the pan in the oven so that the front of the pan is now turned to the back, and check to see if the bottoms are browning too quickly. If so, slide another baking pan underneath to add insulation and retard browning. Continue baking another 7 to 9 minutes until the biscuits are light golden brown. When the biscuits are done, remove from the oven and lightly brush the tops with softened or melted butter. Turn the biscuits out upside down on a plate to cool slightly. Serve hot, right side up.

Prepare the cheese.

VARIATION: CHEESE BISCUITS

Cheddar, Gruyere or Swiss, and blue cheese are also used to make these biscuits.

Benne Seed Biscuits

Makes 36 to 40 (2-inch) biscuits

Edna Lewis was a dear friend for many years. I met her when she was the cook at Middleton Plantation outside Charleston. We spent hours talking about food and life. I include these in homage to her.

1 cup benne (sesame) seeds

3¼ cups all-purpose flour, divided

1½ teaspoons baking powder

1 teaspoon salt

⅓ cup chilled lard, roughly cut into ¼-inch pieces
AND
⅓ cup chilled lard, roughly cut into ½-inch pieces

1 cup milk, divided

Salt, for finish

Preheat oven to 425 degrees F.

Toast the benne seeds on a shallow baking pan in the preheated oven for 5 minutes. Watch carefully for 1 to 2 additional minutes until the seeds turn the color of butterscotch.

Fork-sift or whisk 3 cups of flour, baking powder, and salt in a large bowl, preferably wider than it is deep, and set aside the remaining ¼ cup of flour. Scatter the ¼-inch-size pieces of chilled lard over the flour and work in by rubbing fingers with the fat and flour as if snapping thumb and fingers together (or use two forks or knives, or a pastry cutter) until the mixture looks like well-crumbled feta cheese. Scatter the ½-inch-size pieces of chilled lard over the flour mixture and continue snapping thumb and fingers together until no pieces remain larger than a pea. Shake the bowl occasionally to allow the larger pieces of fat to bounce to the top of the flour, revealing the largest lumps that still need rubbing. If this method took longer than 5 minutes, place the bowl in the refrigerator for 5 minutes to rechill the fat.

Make a deep hollow in the center of the flour with the back of your hand. Pour the milk into the hollow, reserving ⅓ cup, and stir with a rubber spatula or large metal spoon, using broad circular strokes to quickly pull the flour into the milk. Add the toasted benne seeds and mix just until the dry ingredients are moistened and the sticky dough begins to pull away from the sides of the bowl. If there is some flour remaining on the bottom and sides of the bowl, stir in 1 to 4 tablespoons of reserved milk, just enough to incorporate the remaining flour into the shaggy wettish dough. If the dough is too wet, use more flour when shaping.

Lightly sprinkle a board or other clean surface with some of the reserved flour. Turn the dough out onto the board and sprinkle the top lightly with flour. With floured hands, fold the dough in half, and pat dough out into a ⅓- to ½-inch-thick round, using a little additional flour only if needed. Flour again if necessary, and fold the dough in half a second time. If the dough is still clumpy, pat and fold a third time. Pat dough into a ¼-inch-thick round (Miss Edna called it a "nickel-thick round"). Brush off any visible flour from the top. For each biscuit, dip a 2-inch biscuit cutter into the reserved flour and cut out the biscuits, starting at the outside edge and cutting very close together, being careful not to twist the cutter. The scraps may be combined to make additional biscuits, although these scraps make tougher biscuits. For hand-shaping and other variations, see pages 24–26.

Using a metal spatula if necessary, move the biscuits to an ungreased baking sheet. Bake the biscuits on the top rack of the oven for a total of 10 to 14 minutes, depending on thickness, until light golden brown. After 6 minutes, rotate the pan in the oven so that the front of the pan is now turned to the back, and check to see if the bottoms are browning too quickly. If so, slide another baking pan underneath to add insulation and retard browning. Continue baking another 4 to

8 minutes until the biscuits are light golden brown. When the biscuits are done, remove from the oven and sprinkle the top of the biscuits with salt. Turn the biscuits out upside down on a plate to cool slightly. Serve hot, right side up.

Roast benne seeds on a shallow pan.

Cracklin' Cat's Head Biscuits

Makes 14 to 16 (3-inch) biscuits

Cracklings, delicious bits of crisp pork skin, are a typical addition to biscuits, particularly large ones like Cat's Heads, and have a manly appeal. These are seen a great deal during the autumn barbecuing season. Sarah Gaede developed this recipe for The Pirates' House Cook Book and makes them in an iron skillet. We've adapted it here. If over-browning is a concern, use a cake pan instead of an iron skillet.

4¼ cups all-purpose flour, divided

2 tablespoons baking powder

1 teaspoon baking soda

1½ tablespoons granulated sugar

1 teaspoon salt

¼ cup chilled butter, roughly cut into ¼-inch pieces
AND
¼ cup chilled butter, roughly cut into ½-inch pieces

¾ cup cracklings

1¾ cups buttermilk, divided

¼ cup melted butter

Preheat oven to 400 degrees F.

Fork-sift or whisk 4 cups of flour, baking powder, baking soda, sugar, and salt in a large bowl, preferably wider than it is deep, and set aside the remaining ¼ cup of flour. Scatter the ¼-inch-size pieces of chilled fat over the flour and work in by rubbing fingers with the fat and flour as if snapping thumb and fingers together (or use two forks or knives, or a pastry cutter) until the mixture looks like well-crumbled feta cheese. Scatter the ½-inch-size pieces of chilled fat over the flour mixture and continue snapping thumb and fingers together until no pieces remain larger than a pea. Shake the bowl occasionally to allow the larger pieces of fat to bounce to the top of the flour, revealing the largest lumps that still need rubbing. If this method took longer than 5 minutes, place the bowl in the refrigerator for 5 minutes to rechill the fat. Mix in the cracklings.

Make a deep hollow in the center of the flour with the back of your hand. Pour 1½ cups of buttermilk into the hollow, reserving ¼ cup, and stir with a rubber spatula or large metal spoon, using broad circular strokes to quickly pull the flour into the buttermilk. Mix just until the dry ingredients are moistened and the sticky dough begins to pull away from the sides of the bowl. If there is some flour remaining on the bottom and sides of the bowl, stir in 1 to 4 tablespoons of reserved milk, just enough to incorporate the remaining flour into the shaggy wettish dough. If the dough is too wet, use more flour when shaping.

Lightly sprinkle a board or other clean surface with some of the reserved flour. Turn the dough out onto the board and sprinkle the top lightly with flour. With floured hands, fold the dough in half, and pat dough out into a ⅓- to ½-inch-thick round, using a little additional flour only if needed. Flour again if necessary, and fold the dough in half a second time. If the dough is still clumpy, pat and fold a third time. Pat dough out into a ½-inch-thick round for a normal biscuit, ¾-inch-thick for a tall biscuit, and 1-inch-thick for a giant biscuit. Brush off any visible flour from the top. For each biscuit, dip a 3-inch biscuit cutter into the reserved flour and cut out the biscuits, starting at the outside edge and cutting very close together, being careful not to twist the cutter. The scraps may be combined to make additional biscuits, although these scraps make tougher biscuits. For hand-shaping and other variations, see pages 24–26.

Using a metal spatula if necessary, move the biscuits to a 12-inch iron skillet. Pour melted butter over the biscuits and bake on the top rack of the oven for a total of 20 to 25 minutes, depending on thickness, until light golden brown. After 12 minutes, rotate the pan in the oven so that the front of the pan is now turned to the back, and check to see if the bottoms are browning too quickly. If so, slide another baking pan underneath to add insulation and retard browning. Continue baking another 8 to 13 minutes until the biscuits are light golden brown. When the biscuits are done, remove from the oven and turn the biscuits out upside down on a plate to cool slightly. Serve hot, right side up.

Kate Almand is the mother of Georgia biscuits in my experience. From the moment I met her in 1970, I watched her make biscuits, always mesmerized by the motion and beauty of her hands in the wooden bowl of snowy flour. Kate never measures her ingredients for biscuits—she knows automatically how much to use for how many biscuits. Her method is counterintuitive as she combines the shortening and milk before incorporating the flour.

She started making biscuits for her family as a five-year-old girl when her mother was in the hospital. Her father told her how to make biscuits, and she did. Originally, she made small biscuits, perhaps because her parents had twelve children. Her daughter Brenda opened a restaurant, Brenda's, in Social Circle, after I moved away in 2002, saying she was afraid that Kate, well over 70, would get bored after working for me for more than thirty years. Because the customers insisted on a larger biscuit, Kate made hundreds of Cracklin' Cat's Head Biscuits for the restaurant at 5:00 every morning. She retired when she was eightyish.

Parsley Biscuits with Ham and Honey Mustard

Makes 20 (1½-inch) biscuits

These party biscuits should be pop-in-the-mouth tiny to protect fancy clothes and to aid conversation. It is customary to have these biscuits at weddings, receptions, Christmas festivities, New Year's parties, and Easter celebrations. Just about anytime, actually.

2¼ cups commercial or homemade self-rising flour (page 17), divided

2 tablespoons chilled shortening or lard, roughly cut into ¼-inch pieces

2 tablespoons chilled butter roughly cut into ½-inch pieces

½ cup grated imported Parmesan cheese

2 to 3 tablespoons freshly chopped parsley

1 cup buttermilk or whole milk, divided

½ pound thinly sliced ham

Honey Mustard Sauce (page 172)

Preheat oven to 500 degrees F.

Select the baking pan by determining if a soft or crisp exterior is desired. For a soft exterior, use an 8- or 9-inch cake pan, pizza pan, or ovenproof skillet where the biscuits will nestle together snugly, creating the soft exterior while baking. For a crisp exterior, select a baking sheet or other baking pan where the biscuits can be placed wider apart, allowing air to circulate and creating a crisper exterior, and brush the pan with butter.

Fork-sift or whisk 2 cups of flour in a large bowl, preferably wider than it is deep, and set aside the remaining ¼ cup. Scatter the ¼-inch-size pieces of chilled fat over the flour and work in by rubbing fingers with the fat and flour as if snapping thumb and fingers together (or use two forks or knives, or a pastry cutter) until the mixture looks like well-crumbled feta cheese. Scatter the ½-inch-size pieces of chilled fat over the flour mixture and continue snapping thumb and fingers together until no pieces remain larger than a pea. Shake the bowl occasionally to allow the larger pieces of fat to bounce to the top of the flour, revealing the largest lumps that still need rubbing. If this method took longer than 5 minutes, place the bowl in the refrigerator for 5 minutes to rechill the fat. Mix in the Parmesan cheese and parsley.

Make a deep hollow in the center of the flour with the back of your hand. Pour ¾ cup of the buttermilk into the hollow, reserving ¼ cup, and stir with a rubber spatula or large metal spoon, using broad circular strokes to quickly pull the flour into the liquid. Mix just until the dry ingredients are moistened and the sticky dough begins to pull away from the sides of the bowl. If there is some flour remaining on the bottom and sides of the bowl, stir in 1 to 4 tablespoons of reserved milk, just enough to incorporate the remaining flour into the shaggy wettish dough. If the dough is too wet, use more flour when shaping.

Lightly sprinkle a board or other clean surface with some of the reserved flour. Turn the dough out onto the board and sprinkle the top lightly with flour. With floured hands, fold the dough in half, and pat dough out into a ⅓- to ½-inch-thick round, using a little additional flour only if needed. Flour again if necessary, and fold the dough in half a second time. If the dough is still clumpy, pat and fold a third time. Pat dough out into a ½-inch-thick round for a normal biscuit, ¾-inch-thick for a tall biscuit, and 1-inch-thick for a giant biscuit. Brush off any visible flour from the top.

For each biscuit, dip a 1½-inch biscuit cutter into the reserved flour and cut out the biscuits, starting at the outside edge and cutting very close together, being careful not to twist the cutter. The scraps may be combined to make additional biscuits, although these scraps make tougher biscuits. For hand-shaping and other variations, see pages 24–26.

Using a metal spatula if necessary, move the biscuits to the pan or baking sheet. Bake the biscuits on the top rack of the oven for a total 4 to 6 minutes, depending on thickness, until light golden brown. After 3 minutes, rotate the pan in the oven so that the front of the pan is now turned to the back, and check to see if the bottoms are browning too quickly. If so, slide another baking pan underneath to add insulation and slow the browning. Continue baking another 1 to 3 minutes, until the biscuits are light golden brown. When the biscuits are done, remove from the oven and cool completely. Split each biscuit in half and spread with honey mustard, then ham, then other half of biscuit.

Buttermilk Raisin Cinnamon Pecan Biscuits

Makes 20 (2-inch) biscuits

These are nearly like coffee cake, ideal for a morning cup of coffee or tea with a few favorite friends, or a Sunday morning with the family. There are many wonderful kinds of cinnamon out on the market now. Move away from the old faithful and get a real boost in flavor!

2½ cups commercial or homemade self-rising flour (page 17), divided

½ teaspoon ground cinnamon

¼ cup chilled butter, roughly cut into ¼-inch pieces
AND
¼ cup chilled butter, roughly cut into ½-inch pieces

½ cup golden or regular raisins

⅓ cup chopped pecans

1½ cups buttermilk, divided

ICING

½ cup confectioners' sugar

2 tablespoons buttermilk or milk

Preheat oven to 450 degrees F.

Select the baking pan by determining if a soft or crisp exterior is desired. For a soft exterior, use an 8- or 9-inch cake pan, pizza pan, or ovenproof skillet where the biscuits will nestle together snugly, creating the soft exterior while baking. For a crisp exterior, select a baking sheet or other baking pan where the biscuits can be placed wider apart, allowing air to circulate and creating a crisper exterior, and brush the pan with butter.

Fork-sift or whisk 2¼ cups of the flour and cinnamon in a large bowl, preferably wider than it is deep, and set aside the remaining ¼ cup of flour. Scatter the ¼-inch-size pieces of chilled fat over the flour and work in by rubbing fingers with the fat and flour as if snapping thumb and fingers together (or use two forks or knives, or a pastry cutter) until the mixture looks like well-crumbled feta cheese. Scatter the ½-inch-size pieces of chilled fat over the flour mixture and continue snapping thumb and fingers together until no pieces remain larger than a pea. Shake the bowl occasionally to allow the larger pieces of fat to bounce to the top of the flour, revealing the largest lumps that still need rubbing. If this method took longer than 5 minutes, place the bowl in the refrigerator for 5 minutes to rechill the fat. Mix in the raisins and pecans.

Make a deep hollow in the center of the flour with the back of your hand. Pour 1¼ cups of the buttermilk into the hollow, reserving ¼ cup of buttermilk, and stir with a rubber spatula or large metal spoon, quickly pulling the flour into the liquid using broad circular strokes. Mix just until the dry ingredients are moistened and the sticky dough begins to pull away from the sides of the bowl. If there is some flour remaining in the bottom and sides of the bowl, stir in 1 to 4 tablespoons of reserved buttermilk, just enough to incorporate the remaining flour into the shaggy wettish dough. If the dough is too wet, use more flour when shaping.

Lightly sprinkle a board or other clean surface using some of the reserved flour. Turn the dough out onto the board and sprinkle the top of the dough lightly with flour. With floured hands, fold the dough in half, and pat dough out into a ⅓- to ½-inch-thick round, using a little additional flour only if needed. Flour again if necessary, and fold the dough in half a second time. If the dough is still clumpy, pat and fold a third time. Pat dough out into a ½-inch-thick round for a normal biscuit, ¾-inch-thick for a tall biscuit, and 1-inch-thick for a giant biscuit. Brush off any visible flour from the top. For each biscuit, dip a 2-inch biscuit cutter into the reserved flour and cut out the biscuits, starting at the outside edge and cutting very close together, being careful not to twist the cutter. The scraps may be combined to make additional biscuits, although these scraps make tougher biscuits. For hand-shaping and other variations, see pages 24–26.

Using a metal spatula if necessary, move the biscuits to the pan or baking sheet. Bake the biscuits on the top rack of the oven for a total of 12 to 14 minutes, depending on thickness, until light golden brown. After 6 minutes, rotate the pan in the oven so that the front of the pan is now turned to the back, and check to see if the bottoms are browning too quickly. If so, slide another baking pan underneath to add insulation and retard browning. Continue baking another 6 to 8 minutes until the biscuits are light golden brown.

Meanwhile, make the icing by whisking the confectioners' sugar and milk together until smooth. When the biscuits are done, remove from oven and slide them onto a rack over a piece of wax paper. Drizzle the icing over the warm biscuits. Discard the paper with the excess icing. Serve hot right away.

Buttery Blueberry Ginger Biscuits

Makes 16 (2½-inch) biscuits

These skillet-fried biscuits are a little sturdier
than many other biscuits in order to hold
the fresh berries intact. The butter bumps up
the flavor as well. When they are fried, they
remind me of the blueberries we picked early
one morning as Girl Scouts and made into
pancakes—a culinary highlight of my childhood.
But they are very special baked as well. Either
way, they're a winner.

2¼ cups all-purpose flour, divided

1 teaspoon baking powder

1 tablespoon granulated sugar (optional)

¼ teaspoon salt

¼ cup chilled butter, roughly
cut into ¼-inch pieces
AND
¼ cup chilled butter, roughly
cut into ½-inch pieces

1 cup buttermilk, divided

¾ cup fresh blueberries

1 tablespoon crystallized ginger,
finely chopped (optional)

2 to 4 tablespoons melted butter, as needed

Confectioners' sugar (optional)

Softened butter, for brushing

Fork-sift or whisk 2 cups of flour, baking powder, sugar, and salt in a large bowl, preferably wider than it is deep, and set aside the remaining ¼ cup of flour. Scatter the ¼-inch-size pieces of chilled fat over the flour and work in by rubbing fingers with the fat and flour as if snapping thumb and fingers together (or use two forks or knives, or a pastry cutter) until the mixture looks like well-crumbled feta cheese. Scatter the ½-inch-size pieces of chilled fat over the flour mixture and continue snapping thumb and fingers together until no pieces remain larger than a pea. Shake the bowl occasionally to allow the larger pieces of fat to bounce to the top of the flour, revealing the largest lumps that still need rubbing. If this method took longer than 5 minutes, place the bowl in the refrigerator for 5 minutes to rechill the fat.

Make a deep hollow in the center of the flour with the back of your hand. Pour ¾ cup of buttermilk into the hollow, reserving ¼ cup, and stir with a rubber spatula or large metal spoon, using broad circular strokes to quickly pull the flour into the liquid. Mix just until the dry ingredients are moistened and the sticky dough begins to pull away from the sides of the bowl. If there is some flour remaining on the bottom and sides of the bowl, stir in 1 to 4 tablespoons of reserved milk, just enough to incorporate the remaining flour into the shaggy wettish dough. If the dough is too wet, use more flour when shaping.

Lightly sprinkle a board or other clean surface with some of the reserved flour. Turn the dough out onto the board and sprinkle the top lightly with flour. With floured hands, fold the dough in half, and pat dough out into a ⅓- to ½-inch-thick round, using a little additional flour only if needed. Flour again if necessary, and fold the dough in half a second time. If the dough is still clumpy, pat and fold a third time. Pat dough out into a ½-inch-thick round for a normal biscuit, ¾-inch-thick for a tall biscuit, and 1-inch-thick for a giant biscuit. Brush off any visible flour from the top. For each biscuit, dip a 2½-inch biscuit cutter into the reserved flour and cut out the biscuits, starting at the outside edge and cutting very close together, being careful not to twist the cutter. The scraps may be combined to make additional biscuits, although these scraps make tougher biscuits. For hand-shaping and other variations, see pages 24–26.

Toss the blueberries with the ginger. Push 6 blueberries into each biscuit round; don't allow the blueberries to touch each other.

To skillet-fry, heat an iron skillet until hot and add the melted butter. Using a metal spatula, move the biscuits to the skillet. Cook 2 minutes or until lightly browned on the bottom. Turn the biscuits over with the spatula and cook an additional 2 minutes. Remove to a plate and sprinkle with confectioners' sugar if desired.

To bake, preheat oven to 425 degrees F. Move the biscuits to a greased cake pan and bake them on the top rack of the oven for a total of 10 to 14 minutes until light golden brown. After 6 minutes, rotate the pan in the oven so that the front of the pan is now turned to

the back, and check to see if the bottoms are browning too quickly. If so, slide another baking pan underneath to add insulation and retard browning. Continue baking another 4 to 8 minutes until the biscuits are light golden brown. When the biscuits are done, remove from the oven and lightly brush the tops with softened or melted butter. Turn the biscuits out upside down on a plate to cool slightly. Serve hot, right side up, and sprinkle with confectioners' sugar if desired.

VARIATIONS: Peaches, raspberries, blackberries, and other soft fruits (cut blueberry-sized if necessary) do beautifully in this recipe as well. Candied ginger or cinnamon are happy in the biscuits as well.

VARIATION: GREEN ONION BISCUIT

Melt 2 tablespoons butter in a 10-inch skillet over low heat. Evenly distribute 1 teaspoon granulated sugar and ½ of a sliced green onion. Pat biscuits into the skillet, overlapping the biscuits slightly. Sprinkle with more sliced green onion. Cover skillet and cook 5 minutes over medium heat. Turn biscuits over with a pancake turner. Add 2 more tablespoons butter. Cover and cook 5 minutes longer. Serve warm.

Cranberry-Orange Biscuits

Makes 10 (2-inch) biscuits

This recipe, adapted from an old recipe in a Better Homes and Garden cookbook, is a beloved recipe of mine. It just tastes so good, and children and grown-ups all love it. Since it was written by a national publication, a national flour like Pillsbury or Gold Medal may be used. If using Southern flour, you will need 2 to 4 teaspoons more flour. The English call this kind of a scone a "fly" scone because the dried fruit resembles flies.

2¼ cups all-purpose flour, divided

1 tablespoon granulated sugar

2 teaspoons baking powder

¼ teaspoon baking soda

1 teaspoon grated orange rind, no white attached

¼ teaspoon salt

¼ cup chilled shortening, roughly cut into ¼-inch pieces
AND
¼ cup chilled shortening, roughly cut into ½-inch pieces

½ cup snipped dried fruit (cranberries, raisins, cherries, or mixed dried fruit bits)

1 (6-ounce) carton orange or vanilla yogurt

¼ cup milk

Orange Glaze (page 173)

Preheat oven to 450 degrees F.

Select the baking pan by determining if a soft or crisp exterior is desired. For a soft exterior, use an 8- or 9-inch cake pan, pizza pan, or ovenproof skillet where the biscuits will nestle together snugly, creating the soft exterior while baking. For a crisp exterior, select a baking sheet or other baking pan where the biscuits can be placed wider apart, allowing air to circulate and creating a crisper exterior, and brush the pan with butter.

Fork-sift or whisk 2 cups of flour, sugar, baking powder, baking soda, orange rind, and salt in a large bowl, preferably wider than it is deeper, and set aside the remaining ¼ cup of flour. Scatter the ¼-inch-size pieces of chilled fat over the flour and work in by rubbing fingers with the fat and flour as if snapping thumb and fingers together (or use two forks or knives, or a pastry cutter) until the mixture looks like well-crumbled feta cheese. Scatter the ½-inch-size pieces of chilled fat over the flour mixture and continue snapping thumb and fingers together until no pieces remain larger than a pea. Shake the bowl occasionally to allow the larger pieces of fat to bounce to the top of the flour, revealing the largest lumps that still need rubbing. Add the dried fruit and toss until the fruit is well-coated. If this method took longer than 5 minutes, place the bowl in the refrigerator for 5 minutes to rechill the fat.

Make a deep hollow in the center of the flour with the back of your hand. Pour the yogurt into the hollow and stir with a rubber spatula or large metal spoon, using broad circular strokes to quickly pull the flour into the yogurt. Mix just until the dry ingredients are moistened and the sticky dough begins to pull away from the sides of the bowl. If there is some flour remaining on the bottom and sides of the bowl, stir in 1 to 4 tablespoons of the milk, just enough to incorporate the remaining flour into the shaggy wettish dough.

Lightly sprinkle a board or other clean surface with some of the reserved flour. Turn the dough out onto the board and sprinkle the top lightly with flour. With floured hands, fold the dough in half, and pat dough out into a ⅓- to ½-inch-thick round, using a little additional flour only if needed. Flour again if necessary, and fold the dough in half a second time. If the dough is still clumpy, pat and fold a third time. Pat dough out into a ½-inch-thick round for a normal biscuit, ¾-inch-thick for a tall biscuit, and 1-inch-thick for a giant biscuit. Brush off any visible flour from the top. For each biscuit, dip a 2-inch biscuit cutter into the reserved flour and cut out the biscuits, starting at the outside edge and cutting very close together, being careful not to twist the cutter. The scraps may be combined to make additional biscuits, although these scraps make tougher biscuits. For hand-shaping and other variations, see pages 24–26.

Using a metal spatula if necessary, move the biscuits to the pan or baking sheet. Bake the biscuits on the top rack of the oven for a total of 10 to 14 minutes until light golden brown. After 6 minutes, rotate the pan in the oven so that the front of the pan is now turned to the back, and check to see if the bottoms are browning too quickly. If so, slide another baking pan underneath to add insulation and retard browning. Continue baking another 4 to 8 minutes until the biscuits are light golden brown. Turn the biscuits out upside down on a plate to cool slightly. Serve hot, right side up. Drizzle with orange glaze if desired.

Sweet Potato or Pumpkin Biscuits

Makes 18 (2-inch) biscuits

A cup of mashed sweet potatoes or pumpkin guarantees a soft biscuit. The gluten just can't get all worked up, so to speak. They take a little longer to bake than a regular biscuit, but there are more of them for the same amount of other ingredients. Once the shortening or lard is mastered, substitute butter for a very special biscuit.

2¼ cups commercial or homemade self-rising flour (page 17), divided

¼ teaspoon ground cinnamon (optional)

¼ teaspoon ground nutmeg (optional)

⅓ cup chilled shortening or lard, roughly cut into ½-inch pieces

1 cup mashed cooked sweet potatoes or pumpkin purée

¼ cup milk (optional)

ICING

½ cup confectioners' sugar

2 tablespoons buttermilk or milk

Preheat oven to 450 degrees F.

Select the baking pan by determining if a soft or crisp exterior is desired. For a soft exterior, use an 8- or 9-inch cake pan, pizza pan, or ovenproof skillet where the biscuits will nestle together snugly, creating the soft exterior while baking. For a crisp exterior, select a baking sheet or other baking pan where the biscuits can be placed wider apart, allowing air to circulate and creating a crisper exterior, and brush the pan with butter.

Fork-sift or whisk 2 cups of flour, cinnamon, and nutmeg in a large bowl, preferably wider than it is deeper, and set aside the remaining ¼ cup of flour. Scatter lard over the flour and work in by rubbing fingers with the lard and flour as if snapping thumb and fingers together (or use two forks or knives, or a pastry cutter) until the mixture looks like well-crumbled feta cheese, with no piece larger than a pea. Shake the bowl occasionally to allow the larger pieces of fat to bounce to the top of the flour, revealing the largest lumps that still need rubbing. If this method took longer than 5 minutes, place the bowl in the refrigerator for 5 minutes to rechill the fat.

Make a deep hollow in the center of the flour with the back of your hand. Scoop the sweet potatoes into the hollow and stir with a rubber spatula or large metal spoon, using broad circular strokes to quickly pull the flour into the sweet potatoes. Mix just until the dry ingredients are moistened and the sticky dough begins to pull away from the sides of the bowl. If too dry, add 1 to 4 tablespoons of milk.

Lightly sprinkle a board or other clean surface with some of the reserved flour. Turn the dough out onto the board and sprinkle the top lightly with flour. With floured hands, fold the dough in half, and pat dough out into a ⅓- to ½-inch-thick round, using a little additional flour only if needed. Flour again if necessary, and fold the dough in half a second time. If the dough is still clumpy, pat and fold a third time. Pat dough out into a ½-inch-thick round for a normal biscuit, ¾-inch-thick for a tall biscuit, and 1-inch-thick for a giant biscuit. Brush off any visible flour from the top. For each biscuit, dip a 2-inch biscuit cutter into the reserved flour and cut out the biscuits, starting at the outside edge and cutting very close together, being careful not to twist the cutter. The scraps may be combined to make additional biscuits, although these scraps make tougher biscuits. For hand-shaping and other variations, see pages 24–26.

Using a metal spatula if necessary, move the biscuits to the pan or baking sheet. Bake the biscuits on the top rack of the oven for a total of 12 to 14 minutes, depending on thickness, until light golden brown. After 6 minutes, rotate the pan in the oven so that the front of the pan is now turned to the back, and check to see if the bottoms are browning too quickly. If so, slide another baking pan underneath to add insulation and retard browning. Continue baking another 6 to 8 minutes until the biscuits are light golden brown.

Meanwhile, whisk the confectioners' sugar and milk until smooth to make an icing. When the biscuits are done, remove from oven and slide them onto a rack over a piece of wax paper. Drizzle the icing over the warm biscuits. Discard the paper with the excess icing. Serve hot right away.

VARIATION: To make a savory biscuit, omit the optional spices. For bacon biscuits, add ½ cup crumbled cooked bacon before adding the sweet potatoes.

Savory Sweet Potato Biscuits with Ham

On-the-go A.M. Breakfast Sandwich

Makes 8 sandwiches

"Bomber" Biscuits make an excellent package for a breakfast to grab on the run. It is important to do all the chopping and shredding ahead of time so that it just takes a few minutes to cook, and in that time, the biscuits are done.

1 recipe "Bomber" Biscuits (page 68)

6 large eggs

1 teaspoon salt

½ teaspoon freshly ground black pepper

3 tablespoons milk

1 tablespoon butter

¾ cup cooked ham or bacon, chopped

½ cup shredded cheddar cheese

Beat the eggs, salt, pepper, and milk. Melt butter in a skillet, add chopped cooked ham or bacon and sauté over medium heat for 2 minutes. Reduce the heat to low and pour in the egg mixture. Cook until eggs are set, about 5 minutes, stirring occasionally. Stir in cheese and remove from heat. Slice open biscuits and move to a plate or waxed paper. Spoon egg mixture onto the bottom halves of the biscuits. Cover with top halves. If using waxed paper, fold over and wrap for a grab-and-go breakfast.

VARIATION: Add a slice of tomato to each sandwich.

Cynthia did something similar for her daughter Rachel on school mornings and found waxed paper preferable as aluminum foil created steam that made the biscuits a little soggy.

Coca-Cola Biscuits

Makes 10 (2-inch) biscuits

Many a college student will have Coca-Cola around but not milk. These intriguing little biscuits have a flavor that cannot easily be placed. Slightly cocoa-ish, a bit mysterious, but tasty enough to keep an eater interested. They would be delightful baked into a chocolate biscuit bread pudding or simply topped with a smear of Nutella and a toasted marshmallow.

2 cups Homemade Refrigerator Biscuit Mix (page 50) or commercial biscuit mix

¼ cup light or dark brown sugar

½ cup sour cream

½ cup Coca-Cola, divided

Water, if needed

¼ cup all-purpose flour

¼ cup butter, melted

Softened butter, for brushing

Preheat oven to 450 degrees F.

Select the baking pan by determining if a soft or crisp exterior is desired. For a soft exterior, use an 8- or 9-inch cake pan, pizza pan, or ovenproof skillet where the biscuits will nestle together snugly, creating the soft exterior while baking. For a crisp exterior, select a baking sheet or other baking pan where the biscuits can be placed wider apart, allowing air to circulate and creating a crisper exterior, and brush the pan with butter.

Fork-sift or whisk the biscuit mix and brown sugar in a large bowl, preferably wider than it is deep. Make a deep hollow in the center of the mix with the back of your hand. Combine the sour cream and ¼ cup of Coca-Cola in a small bowl. Pour this mixture into the hollow and stir with a rubber spatula or large metal spoon, using broad circular strokes to quickly pull the biscuit mix into the liquid. Add the remaining ¼ cup of Coca-Cola and mix just until the dry ingredients are moistened and the sticky dough begins to pull away from the sides of the bowl. If there is some flour remaining on the bottom and sides of the bowl, stir in 1 to 4 tablespoons water, just enough to incorporate the remaining flour into the shaggy wettish dough. If the dough is too wet, use more flour when shaping.

Lightly sprinkle a board or other clean surface with all-purpose flour. Turn the dough out onto the board and sprinkle the top lightly with flour. With floured hands, fold the dough in half, and pat dough out into a ⅓- to ½-inch-thick round, using a little additional flour only if needed. Flour again if necessary, and fold the dough in half a second time. If the dough is still clumpy, pat and fold a third time. Pat dough out into a 1-inch-thick round. Brush off any visible flour from the top. For each biscuit, dip a 2-inch biscuit cutter into the reserved flour and cut out the biscuits, starting at the outside edge and cutting very close together, being careful not to twist the cutter. The scraps may be combined to make additional biscuits, although these scraps make tougher biscuits. For hand-shaping and other variations, see pages 24–26.

Using a metal spatula if necessary, move the biscuits to the pan or baking sheet. Bake the biscuits on the top rack of the oven for a total of 14 minutes, or until light golden brown. After 7 minutes, rotate the pan in the oven so that the front of the pan is now turned to the back, and check to see if the bottoms are browning too quickly. If so, slide another baking pan underneath to add insulation and retard browning. Continue baking another 7 minutes until the biscuits are light golden brown. When the biscuits are done, remove from the oven and lightly brush the tops with softened or melted butter. Turn the biscuits out upside down on a plate to cool slightly. Serve hot, right side up.

Brush with melted butter.

Half-Dollar Ham Biscuits

Makes 5 dozen

Our friend Barbara Morgan, from Covington, Georgia, is a fabulous cook and entertains frequently. The ham biscuits can, of course, be served as soon as they are made, but when Barbara told me about freezing the biscuits with ham inside for cocktail parties, I was skeptical. After tasting them at Barbara's, however, Cynthia and I agreed they were more than acceptable, and so nice to make ahead. When baking the biscuits, be sure to adjust the recipe to pat the dough ¼-inch thick and cut into 1½-inch rounds.

5 dozen baked 1½-inch Baking Powder Biscuits (page 54), split

¾ cup butter, softened

1 small onion, finely chopped

2 tablespoons poppy seeds

2 to 3 teaspoons Dijon mustard

1 pound thinly shaved ham

Mix together the butter, onion, poppy seeds, and mustard in a small bowl. Spread the bottom halves of the biscuits with the onion mixture. Top with the shaved ham and replace the top halves of the biscuits.

These may be served right away or stored in the refrigerator up to 2 days, tightly wrapped in aluminum foil. To freeze, wrap the biscuits in foil, then in a freezer bag. To reheat, defrost the still-wrapped biscuits in the refrigerator overnight. Reheat biscuits straight from the refrigerator in a 400 degree F oven, still in tightly wrapped foil, until heated through, about 15 minutes.

VARIATION: MONSTER HALF-DOLLAR HAM BISCUITS

Sometimes the temptation is great to serve more meat and let it spill out—as opposed to Barbara's dainty biscuits. See the mouthwatering results on the facing page.

Monster Half-Dollar
Ham Biscuits

Petite Carriage House Biscuits

Makes 60 to 80 (½-inch) biscuits

These dainty biscuits were always promptly served to the ladies' lunch crowd at The Carriage House Restaurant in Natchez, Mississippi, in the days when they were accompanied by frozen fruit salad or tomato aspic. Ever so slightly sweet, they are every bit as good today.

2¼ cups all-purpose flour, divided

¼ teaspoon salt

4 teaspoons baking powder

1 teaspoon sugar

3 tablespoons chilled shortening, roughly cut into ¼-inch pieces
AND
2 tablespoons chilled shortening, roughly cut into ½-inch pieces

1 cup milk, divided

Softened butter, for brushing

Preheat oven to 400 degrees F.

Select the baking pan by determining if a soft or crisp exterior is desired. For a soft exterior, use an 8- or 9-inch cake pan, pizza pan, or ovenproof skillet where the biscuits will nestle together snugly, creating the soft exterior while baking. For a crisp exterior, select a baking sheet or other baking pan where the biscuits can be placed wider apart, allowing air to circulate and creating a crisper exterior, and brush the pan with butter.

Fork-sift or whisk 2 cups of flour, salt, baking powder, and sugar in a large bowl, preferably wider than it is deep, and set aside the remaining ¼ cup of flour. Scatter the ¼-inch-size pieces of chilled fat over the flour and work in by rubbing fingers with the fat and flour as if snapping thumb and fingers together (or use two forks or knives, or a pastry cutter) until the mixture looks like well-crumbled feta cheese. Scatter the ½-inch-size pieces of chilled fat over the flour mixture and continue snapping thumb and fingers together until no pieces remain larger than a pea. Shake the bowl occasionally to allow the larger pieces of fat to bounce to the top of the flour, revealing the largest lumps that still need rubbing. If this method took longer than 5 minutes, place the bowl in the refrigerator for 5 minutes to rechill the fat.

Make a deep hollow in the center of the flour with the back of your hand. Pour ¾ cup of milk into the hollow, reserving ¼ cup, and stir with a rubber spatula or large metal spoon, using broad circular strokes to quickly pull the flour into the milk. Mix just until the dry ingredients are moistened and the sticky dough begins to pull away from the sides of the bowl. If there is some flour remaining on the bottom and sides of the bowl, stir in 1 to 4 tablespoons of reserved milk, just enough to incorporate the remaining flour into the shaggy wettish dough. If the dough is too wet, use more flour when shaping.

Lightly sprinkle a board or other clean surface using some of the reserved flour. Turn the dough out onto the board and sprinkle the top lightly with flour. With floured hands, fold the dough in half, and pat dough out into a ⅓- to ½-inch-thick round, using a little additional flour only if needed. Flour again if necessary, and fold the dough in half a second time. If the dough is still clumpy, pat and fold a third time. Pat dough out into a ¼-inch-thick round. Working from the outside edge in, frequently dip a ½-inch biscuit cutter into the reserved flour and cut out the biscuits without twisting.

The scraps may be combined to make additional biscuits, although these scraps make tougher biscuits.

Using a metal spatula if necessary, move the biscuits to the pan or baking sheet. Bake the biscuits on the top rack of the oven for a total of 15 minutes until light golden brown. After 8 minutes, rotate the pan in the oven so that the front of the pan is now turned to the back, and check to see if the bottoms are browning too quickly. If so, slide another baking pan underneath to add insulation and retard browning. Continue baking another 7 minutes until the biscuits are light golden brown. When the biscuits are done, remove from oven and lightly brush the tops with melted butter. Turn the biscuits out upside down on a plate to cool slightly. Serve hot, right side up.

Senator Hollings' Flaky Appetizer Cream Cheese Biscuits (Carolina Biscuits)

Makes 20 (1-inch) biscuits

U.S. Senator "Fritz" Hollings, one of the truly great raconteurs of the twentieth century, posted this recipe on his website. Also called Carolina Biscuits by some, they are the kind of Southern hors d'oeuvre greedily eaten as opposed to nibbling while standing around drinking and telling stories. Without a doubt the flakiest and richest of all the biscuits we've made, these tiny bites melt in the mouth, need no embellishment, and can be served unadorned, warm out of the oven or at room temperature. As someone said, "I can't believe how good these are." There is no sense doing this by hand when a food processor is available, making it easy and stress-free.

8 ounces cream cheese, softened

⅔ cup butter, softened

1 cup commercial or homemade self-rising flour (page 17), divided

Softened butter, for brushing

Pulse together the cream cheese, ⅔ cup of butter, and 1 cup of the flour two or three times in a food processor fitted with the knife or dough blade. Set aside the ¼ cup of flour and ⅓ cup of butter. Turn the dough out onto waxed paper and divide into two rounds. Wrap in waxed paper, plastic wrap, or a resealable plastic bag, and refrigerate for at least 30 minutes.

When ready to bake, preheat oven to 425 degrees F.

Lightly sprinkle a board or other clean surface using some of the reserved flour. Sprinkle the top lightly with flour. With floured hands and a floured rolling pin, roll out one portion of the dough at a time to approximately ½ inch thick. For each biscuit, dip a 1- to 1¼-inch biscuit cutter into the reserved flour and cut out the biscuits, starting at the outside edge and cutting very close together, being careful not to twist the cutter. The scraps may be combined to make additional biscuits, although these scraps make tougher biscuits. For hand-shaping and other variations, see pages 24–26.

Using a metal spatula if necessary, move the biscuits to an ungreased baking sheet, placing the biscuits 1 inch apart. Bake the biscuits on the top rack of the oven for a total of 10 to 12 minutes until light golden brown. After 6 minutes, rotate the pan in the oven so that the front of the pan is now turned to the back, and check to see if the bottoms are browning too quickly. If so, slide another baking pan underneath to add insulation and retard browning. Continue baking another 4 to 6 minutes until the biscuits are light golden brown. When the biscuits are done, lightly brush the tops with melted butter. Turn the biscuits out upside down on a plate to cool slightly. Serve hot, right side up.

These biscuits may be frozen, unbaked or baked, and reheated.

VARIATION: Press a small spoon into the center of each dough round and insert a ¼ teaspoon of Hot Pepper Jelly (page 176) before or after baking.

Flaky Pecan Party Biscuits

Makes 30 to 40 (1-inch) biscuits

Clara Eschmann was my dear food writer friend from Macon who serendipitously was with us when Jack and I decided to get married in Jamaica, so became my matron of honor. We called each other "cud'n" because we each had a relative that married a relative of the other, cud'n being an affectionate term for an interconnected relationship that cannot be explained.

2¼ cups all-purpose flour, divided

3 teaspoons baking powder

3 tablespoons granulated sugar

½ teaspoon salt

¼ cup chilled butter, roughly cut into ¼-inch pieces
AND
¼ cup chilled butter, roughly cut into ½-inch pieces

½ cup finely chopped pecans

¾ cup milk, divided

1 large egg, slightly beaten

Softened butter, for brushing

Preheat oven to 425 degrees F.

Fork-sift or whisk 2 cups of the flour, baking powder, sugar, and salt in a large bowl; set aside the remaining ¼ cup of flour. Scatter the ¼-inch-size pieces of chilled fat over the flour and work in by rubbing fingers with the fat and flour as if snapping thumb and fingers together (or use two forks or knives, or a pastry cutter) until the mixture looks like well-crumbled feta cheese. Scatter the ½-inch-size pieces of chilled fat over the flour mixture and continue snapping thumb and fingers together until no pieces remain larger than a pea. Shake the bowl occasionally to allow the larger pieces of fat to bounce to the top of the flour, revealing the largest lumps that still need rubbing. If this method took longer than 5 minutes, place the bowl in the refrigerator for 5 minutes to rechill the fat. Stir in the pecans.

Make a deep hollow in the center of the flour with the back of your hand. Lightly beat together ½ cup of milk and egg in a small bowl, reserving ¼ cup of milk. Pour the mixture into the well and stir with a rubber spatula or large metal spoon, using broad circular strokes to quickly pull the flour into the milk. Mix just until the dry ingredients are moistened and the sticky dough begins to pull away from the sides of the bowl. If there is some flour remaining on the bottom and sides of the bowl, stir in 1 to 4 tablespoons of reserved milk, just enough to incorporate the remaining flour into the shaggy wettish dough. If the dough is too wet, use more flour when shaping.

Lightly sprinkle a board or other clean surface using some of the reserved flour. Turn out the dough onto the flour. With floured hands, fold the dough in half, and pat dough out into a $\frac{1}{3}$- to $\frac{1}{2}$-inch-thick round, using a little additional flour only if needed. Flour again if necessary, and fold the dough in half a second time. If the dough is still clumpy, pat and fold a third time. Pat dough out into a $\frac{1}{3}$-inch-thick round. Dip a 1-inch biscuit cutter into the reserved flour and cut out the biscuits, starting at the outside edge and cutting very close together, being careful not to twist the cutter. The scraps may be combined to make additional biscuits, although these scraps make tougher biscuits.

Using a spatula if necessary, move the biscuits to an ungreased baking sheet, touching each other for a soft exterior or separating them for a crispy biscuit. The baking sheet should always be 2 inches smaller than the interior of the oven, providing sufficient space for air circulation.

Bake the biscuits on the top rack of the oven for 12 to 15 minutes until light golden brown. Rotate the pan in the oven after 6 minutes and check to see if the bottoms are browning too quickly. If so, slide another baking pan underneath to add insulation and retard browning. Continue baking another 7 minutes until the biscuits are light golden brown. When the biscuits are done, brush the tops with melted butter. Turn the biscuits out upside down on a plate to cool slightly. Serve hot, right side up.

*Rainy-day Beef Stew and
Thyme Dumplings*

Biscuit Relatives

Biscuit relatives are not exactly biscuits but are variations built on the basic biscuit ingredients. Cheese Straws (page 137) are one of the most popular and enduring favorites in the South. Add a little blue cornmeal to a biscuit and you have something fit for a southwestern aficionado—Cheddar-Chipotle Cornmeal Biscuits (page 140). And when biscuit dough is almost a batter, it can be spooned into muffin cups, as seen with Paul Prudhomme's Southern Biscuit Muffins (page 142).

Butter Dips

This is an "after school" treat I remember from the 1950s. As I recall, I just dumped everything together, the result not being as tender and gratifying as these are.

¼ cup butter

1½ cup commercial or homemade self-rising flour (page 17), divided

2 teaspoons granulated sugar

1 cup milk, divided

Cinnamon sugar (optional)

Preheat oven to 450 degrees F.

Melt the butter in a 9-inch square pan in the heated oven and remove. Fork-sift or whisk 1¼ cups of flour and sugar in a large bowl, preferably wider than it is deep, and set aside the remaining ¼ cup of flour. Make a deep hollow in the center of the flour with the back of your hand. Pour ⅔ cup of milk into the hollow, reserving ⅓ cup, and stir with a rubber spatula or large metal spoon, using broad circular strokes to quickly pull the flour into the milk. Mix just until the dry ingredients are moistened and the sticky dough begins to pull away from the sides of the bowl. If there is some flour remaining on the bottom and sides of the bowl, stir in 1 to 4 tablespoons of additional milk, just enough to incorporate the remaining flour into the shaggy wettish dough. If the dough is too wet, use more flour when shaping.

Lightly sprinkle a board or other clean surface with some of the reserved flour. Turn the dough out onto the board and sprinkle the top lightly with flour. With floured hands, fold the dough in half, and pat dough out into a ⅓- to ½-inch-thick round, using a little additional flour only if needed. Flour again if necessary, and fold the dough in half a second time. If the dough is still clumpy, pat and fold a third time. Pat dough out into an 8-inch square. Cut the dough in half, and then cut each half into 9 (4-inch) strips. Dip each strip into the melted butter, coating both sides, and place close together in the prepared pan. Bake on the top rack of the oven for a total of 15 to 20 minutes until light golden brown. When the dips are done, remove from the oven, sprinkle with cinnamon sugar, if using, and cool briefly. Serve warm.

Cheese Straws or Wafers

Makes 3 to 4 dozen using the cookie press, or 2 dozen (6-inch) straws

Cheese straws are as Southern as boiled peanuts, but a lot easier to eat. They are crisp, buttery and cheesy, but have a zing from the red pepper that stays just a second at the end, making a person reach for another. I try to keep these on hand for drop-in friends and last-minute needs, but unfortunately, they just keep getting eaten up too fast to keep up with making them!

1 ½ cups Homemade Refrigerator Biscuit Mix (page 50) or commercial biscuit mix

1 ½ cups grated sharp cheddar cheese

½ cup butter, roughly cut into ½-inch pieces

1 tablespoon Dijon mustard

⅛ teaspoon ground red pepper (cayenne)

½ to 1 teaspoon salt

Preheat oven to 375 degrees F.

Pulse together the biscuit mix, cheese, butter, mustard, and pepper in a food processor fitted with the knife or dough blade. Pulse until dough just begins to pull together into a ball, being careful not to over-process.

At this point there are many ways to shape the dough:

Option 1: Move to a sheet of wax paper. Cover dough with another sheet of wax paper and roll to ¼-inch thick. Refrigerate dough 15 minutes, still between wax paper. Remove top sheet and, using a pastry wheel or knife, cut dough into ¾-inch wide strips.

Option 2: Divide dough in half, and turn out each half onto plastic wrap that is twice as long as the dough ball. With both hands, press and roll the dough into a 2-inch-wide cylinder. Pinch and twist the ends until it looks like a large Tootsie Roll. Chill until firm and slice into wafers.

Option 3: Scoop a portion of the dough into a cookie press with the desired cut-shape attached to the press, keeping unused portion refrigerated.

Move shapes 1 inch apart on an ungreased baking sheet. Bake for 8 to 10 minutes. Once the aroma comes wafting out of the oven, they are usually done. Cooking further may burn the cheese. Remove with a metal spatula to cool on a rack. These will keep several days in a tightly wrapped container or may be frozen, for up to 3 months. If necessary, re-crisp soggy ones on a pan in a 300 degree F oven.

Blue Cornmeal Biscuits

Makes 14 (2½-inch) biscuits

Cornbread, like biscuits, is a Southern staple. It is always a difficult choice to make at a meal: cornbread or biscuits? Rather than deciding between the two, why not combine them into one delectable treat that is as welcome at breakfast as it is alongside a hearty bowl of chili? Hayley Daen brought in the blue cornmeal and the idea one day, and whipped these up. I love cornmeal, and I would do this with any color cornmeal and revel in them. But truly, the blue ones are a conversation stopper.

1½ cups commercial or homemade
self-rising flour (page 17)

1¼ cups blue cornmeal, divided

1 tablespoon light or dark brown sugar

¼ cup butter, roughly cut into ½-inch pieces

1¼ cups milk, divided

Softened butter, for brushing

Preheat oven to 425 degrees F.

Select the baking pan by determining if a soft or crisp exterior is desired. For a soft exterior, use an 8- or 9-inch cake pan, pizza pan, or oven-proof skillet where the biscuits will nestle together snugly, creating the soft exterior while baking. For a crisp exterior, select a baking sheet or other baking pan where the biscuits can be placed wider apart, allowing air to circulate and creating a crisper exterior, and brush the pan with butter.

Fork-sift or whisk the 1¼ cups of flour, 1 cup of cornmeal, and sugar in a large bowl, preferably wider than deep, and set aside the remaining ¼ cup of flour and ¼ cup of cornmeal. Scatter the butter over the flour and work in by rubbing fingers with the butter and flour as if snapping thumb and fingers together (or use two forks or knives, or a pastry cutter) until the mixture looks like well-crumbled feta cheese, with no piece larger than a pea. Shake the bowl occasionally to allow the larger pieces of fat to bounce to the top of the flour, revealing the largest lumps that still need rubbing. If this method took longer than 5 minutes, place the bowl in the refrigerator for 5 minutes to rechill the fat.

Make a deep hollow in the center of the flour with the back of your hand. Pour 1 cup of milk into the hollow, reserving ¼ cup, and stir the milk, using broad circular strokes to quickly pull the flour mixture into the milk. Mix just until the dry ingredients are moistened and the sticky dough begins to pull away from the sides of the bowl. If there is some flour remaining on the bottom and sides of the bowl, stir in 1 to 4 tablespoons of reserved milk, just enough to incorporate the remaining flour into the dough.

Lightly sprinkle a board or other clean surface with some of the reserved cornmeal. Turn the dough out onto the cornmeal and sprinkle the top lightly with cornmeal. With floured hands, fold the dough in half, and pat dough out into a ⅓- to ½-inch-thick round, using a little additional flour only if needed. Flour again if necessary, and fold the dough in half a second time. If the dough is still clumpy, pat and fold a third time. Pat dough out into a ½-inch-thick round for a normal biscuit, ¾-inch-thick for a tall biscuit, and 1-inch-thick for a giant biscuit. For each biscuit, dip a 2½-inch biscuit cutter into the reserved flour and cut out the biscuits, starting at the outside edge and cutting very close together, being careful not to twist the cutter. The scraps may be combined to make additional biscuits, although these scraps make tougher biscuits. For hand-shaping and other variations, see pages 24–26.

Using a metal spatula if necessary, move the biscuits to the pan or baking sheet. Bake the biscuits on the top rack of the oven for a total of 10 minutes until light golden brown. After 6 minutes, rotate the pan in the oven so that the front of the pan is now turned to the back, and check to see if the bottoms are browning too quickly. If so, slide another baking pan underneath to add insulation and retard browning. Continue baking another 4 minutes until the biscuits are light golden brown. When the biscuits are done, remove from the oven and lightly brush the tops with softened or melted butter. Turn the biscuits out upside down on a plate to cool slightly. Serve hot, right side up.

VARIATIONS: Use white or yellow cornmeal in place of the blue cornmeal. For a sky-high rise, use self-rising cornmeal.

Cheddar-Chipotle Cornmeal Biscuits

Makes 10 (3-inch) biscuits

"Zing" and "zip" are the perfect words to describe these biscuits with their tangy cheddar and spicy chilies. The combination of cornmeal and flour makes a semi-cornbread/semi-biscuit, very satisfying and hearty, good for dipping in turnip green pot likker or a beef chili.

1 to 2 tablespoons butter

½ cup chopped green onions
or scallions, green only

1¾ cups all-purpose flour, divided

½ cup cornmeal, preferably yellow

2 tablespoons granulated sugar

2½ teaspoons baking powder

½ teaspoon baking soda

½ teaspoon salt

½ cup chilled butter, roughly
cut into ½-inch pieces

1½ cups coarsely grated sharp cheddar cheese

1 cup buttermilk, divided

2 large eggs

1 tablespoon finely minced canned chipotle
chiles in adobo, or 1 tablespoon fresh
or dried hot red peppers (optional)

1 tablespoon whipping cream

Preheat oven to 425 degrees F.

Melt the butter in a frying pan over medium-high heat; when hot, add the green onions and cook for about 5 minutes, until slightly soft. Set aside.

Pulse together 1½ cups of flour, cornmeal, sugar, baking powder, baking soda, and salt in a food processor. Set aside the ¼ cup of flour. Scatter the butter over the flour mixture and pulse until mixture resembles well-crumbled feta cheese, with no piece larger than a pea. Add cheese and pulse briefly to incorporate. Move the flour mixture to a large bowl.

Whisk together ¾ cup of buttermilk, reserving ¼ cup, and 1 egg in a medium bowl. Stir in the cooked green onions and 1 tablespoon of the optional chiles or peppers.

Make a deep hollow in the center of the flour with the back of your hand. Pour the buttermilk mixture into the hollow and stir with a rubber spatula or large metal spoon, using broad circular strokes to quickly pull the flour into the liquid. Mix just until the dry ingredients are moistened and the sticky dough begins to pull away from the sides of the bowl. If there is some flour remaining on the bottom and sides of the bowl, stir in 1 to 4 tablespoons of reserved buttermilk, just enough to incorporate the remaining flour into the shaggy dough.

Lightly sprinkle a board or other clean surface with some of the reserved flour. Turn the dough out onto the board and sprinkle the top lightly with flour. With floured hands, fold the dough in half, and pat dough out into a ⅓- to ½-inch-thick round, using a little additional flour only if needed. Flour again if necessary, and fold the dough in half a second time. If the dough is still clumpy, pat and fold a third time. Pat dough out into a ¾-inch-thick round. Brush off any visible flour from the top. For each biscuit, dip a 3-inch biscuit cutter into the reserved flour and cut out the biscuits, starting at the outside edge and cutting very close together, being careful not to twist the cutter. Combine the scraps to make additional biscuits.

Using a metal spatula if necessary, move the biscuits to an ungreased baking sheet, placing the biscuits 1 inch apart. Whisk together the remaining egg and cream to make a glaze. Brush the biscuits with the glaze and bake on the top rack of the oven for a total of 18 minutes until light golden brown and a toothpick inserted in the center of a biscuit comes out clean. Cool the biscuits on a rack for 5 minutes. Serve warm.

Paul Prudhomme's Southern Biscuit Muffins

Makes 12 muffins

Chef Paul Prudhomme is a generous cook, and this adaptation of his buttery biscuit muffins exemplifies that. Muffin cups are necessary for these biscuits.

2¾ cups all-purpose flour, divided

¼ cup granulated sugar

1½ tablespoons baking powder

¼ teaspoon salt

½ cup chilled butter,
roughly cut into ¼-inch pieces
AND
½ cup plus 2 tablespoons chilled butter,
roughly cut into ½-inch pieces

1¼ cups milk, divided

APOQUINIMINC CAKES

Put a little salt, one egg beaten, and four ounces of butter, in a quart of flour—make it into a paste with new milk, beat it for half an hour with a pestle, roll the paste thin and cut into round cakes; bake them on a gridiron, and be careful not to burn them.

—*The Virginia Housewife*,
Mary Randolph, 1824

Preheat oven to 350 degrees F.

Fork-sift or whisk 2½ cups of flour, sugar, baking powder, and salt in a large bowl, preferably wider than it is deep, and set aside the remaining ¼ cup of flour. Scatter the ¼-inch-size pieces of chilled fat over the flour and work in by rubbing fingers with the fat and flour as if snapping thumb and fingers together (or use two forks or knives, or a pastry cutter) until the mixture looks like well-crumbled feta cheese. Scatter the ½-inch-size pieces of chilled fat over the flour mixture and continue snapping thumb and fingers together until no pieces remain larger than a pea. Shake the bowl occasionally to allow the larger pieces of fat to bounce to the top of the flour, revealing the largest lumps that still need rubbing. If this method took longer than 5 minutes, place the bowl in the refrigerator for 5 minutes to rechill the fat.

Make a deep hollow in the center of the flour with the back of your hand. Pour 1 cup of milk into the hollow, reserving ¼ cup, and stir with a rubber spatula or large metal spoon, using broad circular strokes to quickly pull the flour into the milk. Mix just until the dry ingredients are moistened and the sticky dough begins to pull away from the sides of the bowl. If there is some flour remaining on the bottom and sides of the bowl, stir in 1 to 4 tablespoons of reserved milk, just enough to incorporate the remaining flour into the shaggy wettish dough.

Spoon the dough into greased muffin cups. Bake 35 to 40 minutes until golden brown. The finished muffins should have a thick crust with a cake-like center.

Buttermilk Rusks

Makes 6 very large rusks

For the people who like the corners of a brownie,
the heel of a loaf of bread, or the browned edges
of a crispy cookie, rusks are heaven. They are not
intensely flavorful, but their crunch is delightful,
and their quiet sweetness makes it justifiable to
eat so many. They are just as nice a spread with
jam or another tasty topping as they are dipped
in hot coffee or tea.

3 cups commercial or homemade
self-rising flour (page 17)

⅓ cup granulated sugar

6 tablespoons butter, room
temperature, cut into small pieces

1 cup buttermilk, plus 1 tablespoon for glazing

1 tablespoon vanilla extract

1 large egg, lightly beaten

Preheat oven to 350 degrees F.

Fork-sift or whisk the flour and sugar in a large bowl,
preferably wider than deep. Scatter the butter over the flour
and work in by rubbing your fingers with the butter and flour
as if snapping thumb and fingers together (or use two forks
or knives, or a pastry cutter) until the mixture looks like well-
crumbled feta cheese, with no piece larger than a pea. Shake
the bowl occasionally to allow the larger pieces of fat to
bounce to the top of the flour, revealing the largest lumps that
still need rubbing. Whisk 1 cup buttermilk, vanilla, and egg
together in a small bowl. Make a deep hollow in the center
of the flour with the back of your hand. Pour the buttermilk
mixture into the hollow and stir, using broad circular strokes
to quickly pull the flour into the wet ingredients. Mix just
until the dry ingredients are moistened and the sticky dough
begins to pull away from the sides of the bowl.

With floured hands, divide the dough into 8 pieces. Roll each
piece into a ball and set the balls of dough in a large loaf pan
or small casserole dish (preferably 9 x 5 x 2¾ inches) so that
the sides of each rusk touch one another. Brush each of the
rusks with the remaining tablespoon of buttermilk. Bake for
30 minutes; reduce the heat to 300 degrees F, and bake for an
additional 30 minutes. Remove the loaf pan and turn out the
rusks, which have spread slightly into what look like large
dinner rolls, onto a wire rack. Move the rusks to a parchment-
lined baking sheet and bake for 2 hours at 200 degrees F.
Allow to cool slightly. To serve, spread with butter and
sprinkle with cinnamon sugar, or slather with Nutella.

Mrs. Dull's 5 O'Clock Tea Porter Puffs

Makes 60 puffs

This is perhaps the most decadent of Mrs. Dull's biscuit recipes, kind of a sweet popover biscuit. I can hardly visualize her deciding to pour a teaspoon of butter in each of these, but I can picture how wonderful it was to eat them as they are so delicious. Cynthia and I ate half a dozen puffs each, oozing with butter, when we made them together. We decided surely if it wasn't Mrs. Dull's recipe, it would definitely be a sin to eat them. I live in Charleston where 5 o'clock tea is rare. But in the winter, with a fire—well, why not sin a little?

1 large egg

1 cup milk

2 tablespoons granulated sugar

2 cups commercial or homemade self-rising flour (page 17)

1 cup melted butter, divided

Confectioners' sugar (optional)

Preheat oven to 450 degrees F.

Heat a well-greased (not buttered) mini muffin tin in the oven until hot.

Whisk together the egg and milk in a large bowl. Stir in the sugar and enough of the flour to make a very thick batter. Stir in ¼ cup of melted butter. Reserve remaining melted butter in a small pitcher with a pointed spout, if possible, and keep warm on the stove.

Drop a heaping teaspoonful of batter into each sizzling hot muffin cup, filling each about half full. Quickly move the muffin tin to the oven while still hot. Bake until brown and puffed, about 10 minutes depending on size. Remove from oven and turn out the puffs onto a plate. Puncture the side of each muffin with the spout of the pitcher, pour about a teaspoon of melted butter into the muffin, and serve at once. Better use plates! Oh, and if you want an additional sin to confess, sprinkle with confectioners' sugar.

VARIATION: Mix a little water with your favorite jam and pour into the puff in the same manner as the butter. Chocolate Gravy (page 180) is another option.

Cheese Sausage Pinwheels

Makes 24 pinwheels

Cheese biscuit dough spread with cooked sausage, then rolled and sliced into dizzyingly beautiful rounds before baking makes a wonderful nibble anytime a savory snack is desired. This may be made from any sturdy buttermilk or whole milk dough, but is particularly good with the Food Processor Golden Cheese Biscuits (page 77).

1 recipe Food Processor Golden Cheese Biscuits (page 77), before cutting

1 (16-ounce) roll mild or hot sausage, lightly cooked

Preheat oven to 400 degrees F.

Pat the dough onto a floured surface into a 14 x 10-inch rectangle, about ¼ inch thick. Crumble the lightly cooked sausage evenly over the biscuit dough. Starting on a long side of the rectangle, use the heel of one hand and roll the dough up in jelly-roll style. Slice the roll into ½-inch-wide pinwheels. Move to a baking sheet and bake 15 to 18 minutes until lightly browned.

VARIATION: CHEESE WHEELS

Roll out biscuit dough to ¼ inch thickness. Spread generously with grated cheese, sprinkle with red pepper, and roll up like a jelly roll. Slice the roll into ½-inch-wide pinwheels, place on greased baking sheet, and bake in moderate oven until done and brown. They are good hot or cold. Leave space on the baking sheet for biscuits to spread.

MRS. DULL'S BISCUIT FRITTERS

Use recipe for biscuit made with sweet milk. Roll out dough thin, cut with large cutter, place spoonful of jam or stewed fruit on one-half, wet the edge, cover with other half, press together with fork or fingers, fry in deep fat, drain, sprinkle with powdered sugar.

—*Southern Cooking*, Mrs. S. R. Dull, 1928

Buttermilk Coffee Cake

Makes 18 pieces

This is get-out-of-the-bed enticing. It will bring teenagers downstairs on Saturday mornings, it's that good. It totes well, it freezes, it's yummy.

2½ cups all-purpose flour

1½ cups packed light or dark brown sugar

½ teaspoon salt

⅔ cup chilled butter, roughly cut into ½-inch pieces

2 large eggs, lightly beaten

1⅓ cups buttermilk

2 teaspoons baking powder

½ teaspoon baking soda

½ teaspoon ground cinnamon

½ teaspoon ground nutmeg

½ cup chopped pecans

Preheat oven to 350 degrees F. Grease the bottom and sides of a 9 x 13-inch baking dish and set aside.

Fork-sift or whisk the flour, brown sugar, and salt in a large bowl, preferably wider than it is deep. Scatter the butter over the flour and work in by rubbing fingers with the butter and flour as if snapping thumb and fingers together (or use two forks or knives, or a pastry cutter) until the mixture looks like well-crumbled feta cheese, with no piece larger than a pea. Remove ½ cup of the flour mixture to a small bowl and set aside.

Make a deep hollow in the center of the flour with the back of your hand. Lightly beat the eggs into the buttermilk, pour mixture into the hollow, and stir with a rubber spatula or large metal spoon, using broad circular strokes to quickly pull the flour into the buttermilk mixture. Mix just until the dry ingredients are moistened. Spoon the batter into the prepared baking dish.

Stir the baking powder, baking soda, cinnamon, nutmeg, and pecans into the reserved flour mixture. Sprinkle over the batter.

Bake 35 to 40 minutes until a toothpick inserted in the center comes out clean. Remove from the oven and let cool for 10 minutes. Slice into squares and serve warm.

Peach Coffee Cake

Makes 1 (12-cup) Bundt cake

There's not much notice—but after waiting and waiting for fresh peaches, all of a sudden the first clingstones are here! A biscuit mix is a clever and quick way to use the clingstones, which are not very pretty for hand eating, but joyously are the first of the season to ripen. They are also the ones sold commercially as they are so well suited for cooking.

3 cups Homemade Refrigerator Biscuit Mix (page 50) or commercial biscuit mix

¾ cup granulated sugar

2 large eggs

2 teaspoons vanilla extract, divided

¼ cup butter, melted

2 cups sliced fresh or frozen peaches and their juice

1 cup sour cream

½ cup finely chopped pecans

1 cup confectioners' sugar

2 tablespoons water

Preheat oven to 350 degrees F. Grease a Bundt pan and set aside.

Fork-stir or whisk together the biscuit mix and sugar in a large bowl. Stir together the eggs, 1½ teaspoons of vanilla, and butter; pour over biscuit mix. Break up peaches into large chunks and stir into biscuit mixture. Add sour cream and pecans, and stir together until well combined. Pour into prepared pan and bake on the middle rack for 55 minutes, or until a toothpick inserted in the center comes out clean (there may be a few crumbs). Move to a rack and cool 15 minutes. Turn coffee cake out on rack and cool completely. Stir together confectioners' sugar, water, and remaining ½ teaspoon vanilla, and drizzle over cooled coffee cake.

Pancakes

Makes 12 (4-inch) pancakes

Although some form of pancake has been made since earliest times, the addition of baking powder made a fluffier, more tender product. Some people prefer making batter ahead of time, letting it rest 15 minutes or overnight. If time is of the essence, the batter can be cooked immediately. Remember that the first pancake is a test to be sure the griddle is hot. Don't fret, just give it to the dog if it lacks perfection.

1½ cups milk

1 large egg

2 cups Homemade Refrigerator Biscuit Mix (page 50) or commercial biscuit mix

Stir the milk and egg together in a bowl, add the biscuit mix, and stir until just combined. Let the batter rest for 10 minutes. Heat a nonstick skillet or griddle over medium-high heat. For a 4-inch pancake, pour ¼ cup batter onto the hot skillet. Cook until the edges begin to dry and the top begins to show bubbles. Turn and cook 1 to 2 minutes until the underside is golden brown. If the batter starts to thicken as it sits, add a little milk to thin the batter. Serve warm.

VARIATION: BUTTERMILK

As the buttermilk instantly activates the leaveners in the biscuit mix, cook these right away without resting the batter.

Waffles

Makes 12 (4-inch) waffles

Blacksmiths of thirteenth-century Europe are the founders of what we know as a waffle, a batter cooked simultaneously on both sides. The blacksmiths designed intricate coats of arms and other symbols on hinged iron plates attached to wooden handles. Held over an open fire, this method lasted for centuries.

Thomas Jefferson brought one back from France in 1789 and began to host "waffle frolics" that became the rage in all levels of society. The modern electric version was commonplace in the home by 1930. My husband has a treasured heavy electric iron, one I wouldn't dare change.

Like pancake batter, a rest improves the batter, and the first one or two are always tests to be sure the temperature of the waffle iron is right.

1½ cups milk

1 large egg

2 tablespoons butter, melted

2 cups Homemade Refrigerator Biscuit Mix (page 50) or commercial biscuit mix

Stir the milk and egg together. Pour in the melted butter and stir to mix. Add the liquid to the biscuit mix and stir until just combined. Let the batter rest for 10 minutes. Heat a lightly greased waffle iron and pour ½ cup batter into each waffle well. Close the lid and follow manufacturer's directions for cooking time. Do not open the lid until the waffle is done. Use a fork to lift the waffle from the waffle iron. Repeat using remaining batter. If the batter starts to thicken as it sits, add a little milk to thin it. Serve warm.

Chicken or Turkey Biscuit Pot Pie

Serves 4 to 6

A biscuit pot pie is a wonderful make-ahead as well as "leftovers" dish or one using a precooked chicken. The chicken and other ingredients may be made ahead of time, up to two days. When ready to serve, reheat gently and put in a pretty oven-to-table dish or glass pie plate. The biscuits can be made up to two hours ahead. When assembled and cooked just enough to bake the biscuit, a dazzling main course is ready in a short time. All it needs is a salad.

6 tablespoons butter, divided

2 red bell peppers, seeded and sliced thinly (optional)

1 onion, sliced

1 cup sliced mushrooms

4 tablespoons flour

1½ cups chicken stock or broth, fresh or canned

1 to 2 teaspoons chopped fresh herbs such as thyme or oregano (optional)

4 tablespoons heavy cream

3 cups shredded cooked chicken

Salt and freshly ground black pepper

1 recipe Buttermilk Biscuits for Pot Pie (page 152)

Preheat oven to 425 degrees F. Butter a 10-inch oven-to-table or glass pie dish.

Melt 2 to 3 tablespoons of the butter in a large skillet, add the peppers and onion, top with the mushrooms, and cook for several minutes over medium heat until tender.

In a separate pan, melt the remaining 3 or 4 tablespoons of butter and the flour. Stir together until smooth, and then cook slowly until it turns a deep golden brown. Add the stock and bring to the boil, stirring. Add cream, return to the boil, and cook to reduce in quantity. (It should be smooth and free of lumps. If not, strain before adding the solids.) Remove from the heat and add the shredded chicken, optional peppers, onion, and mushrooms. Season to taste with salt and pepper, if using. This may be done up to two days in advance.

Up to two hours before serving, make the biscuits, cut into 1½-inch rounds, and refrigerate if desired. Reheat the chicken mixture before adding to buttered dish. Top mixture with the biscuits, making sure they touch. If it seems too full, slide a baking sheet underneath to catch drips. Move to the hot oven and bake until biscuits are done, about 12 to 14 minutes.

Although this dish may be frozen (tightly wrapped, defrosted in the refrigerator, and reheated), it would be best to freeze the chicken mixture, reheat it, and then top with freshly made biscuit dough.

VARIATION: Add fresh or frozen "English Peas" before topping with biscuit dough.

Buttermilk Biscuits for Pot Pie

There's just no sense in spending a lot of time on a pot pie or its topping. Use butter to complement the flavor of the pie filling and make the dough completely in the food processor. If everything is made in advance, a pot pie can be assembled at the last minute for a superb meal.

2¼ cups commercial or homemade self-rising flour (page 17), divided

¼ cup chilled butter, roughly cut into ¼-inch pieces
AND
¼ cup chilled butter, roughly cut into ½-inch pieces

1 cup buttermilk, divided

Set aside ¼ cup of flour. Pulse 2 cups of flour 2 or 3 times in a food processor fitted with the knife or dough blade. Scatter the ¼-inch butter pieces over the flour mixture and pulse 2 or 3 times. Scatter the ½-inch butter pieces over the flour mixture and pulse 2 or 3 times until mixture resembles well-crumbled feta cheese, with no piece larger than a pea. Add ¾ cup of the buttermilk, reserving ¼ cup, and pulse briefly to incorporate into a shaggy wettish dough. When the blade stops, remove the lid and feel the dough. Add more reserved buttermilk or flour as needed to make a slightly wettish dough. Pulse once or twice more until the dough looks shaggy but together.

Lightly sprinkle a board or other clean surface with some of the reserved flour. Turn the dough out onto the board and sprinkle the top lightly with flour. With floured hands, fold the dough in half, and pat dough out into a ⅓- to ½-inch-thick round, using a little additional flour only if needed. Flour again if necessary, and fold the dough in half a second time. If the dough is still clumpy, pat and fold a third time. Pat dough out into a ½-inch-thick round for a normal biscuit, ¾-inch-thick for a tall biscuit, and 1-inch-thick for a giant biscuit. Brush off any visible flour from the top. Working from the outside edge in, dip a 1½-inch biscuit cutter into the reserved flour frequently and cut out the biscuits without twisting. (Dough rounds can be refrigerated on a lightly floured baking sheet covered with plastic wrap for up to 2 hours.) Arrange dough rounds over warm filling and bake as directed.

Chicken and Drop Dumplings

Chicken soup is truly a soul-warming dish. Chicken and dumplings take that notion to new heights. These drop dumplings are very soft and tend to break up. If a sturdier biscuit dumpling is desired, add more flour. There is also a variation for a pasta-type rolled dumpling.

CHICKEN

3 cups shredded cooked chicken

4 cups chicken stock or broth, fresh or commercial

1 cup milk

Salt

Freshly ground black pepper

DUMPLINGS

1 cup all-purpose flour

1 teaspoon baking powder

1 teaspoon salt

¼ cup chilled shortening, roughly cut into ½-inch pieces

⅓ cup milk

Move the chicken to a heavy Dutch oven. Add the chicken stock, cover, and bring to the boil. Add the milk and return to the boil. Reduce heat to simmer while making the dumplings. Season to taste with salt and pepper.

Fork-sift or whisk the flour, baking powder, and salt in a large bowl, preferably wider than it is deep. Scatter the shortening over the flour and work in by rubbing fingers with the shortening and flour as if snapping thumb and fingers together (or use two forks or knives, or a pastry cutter) until the mixture looks like well-crumbled feta cheese, with no piece larger than a pea. If this method took longer than 5 minutes, place the bowl in the refrigerator for 5 minutes to rechill the fat.

Make a deep hollow in the center of the flour with the back of your hand. Pour the milk into the hollow and stir with a rubber spatula or large metal spoon, using broad circular strokes to quickly pull the flour into the milk. Mix just until the dry ingredients are moistened and the wet dough begins to pull away from the sides of the bowl.

Bring the chicken and broth back up to the boil and drop the dumplings, a teaspoonful at a time, into the boiling broth. Cover, reduce heat, and simmer 10 minutes. The dumplings will swell and break up a bit.

VARIATION: PEPPER DUMPLINGS

Add 1 tablespoon freshly ground black pepper to the dough.

Rainy-day Beef Stew and Thyme Dumplings

Serves 6 to 8

Here is a rarely seen Southern dumpling. It contains an egg, which makes it more like a modern-day scone rather than a Southern dumpling. Any other kind of dumpling (pages 153 and 157) may be used instead.

BEEF STEW

2 tablespoons vegetable oil

½ pound boneless beef, cut into 2-inch pieces

1 onion, chopped

2 large Yukon Gold or other potatoes, cut in large pieces

4 to 6 carrots, peeled and roughly sliced

6 cups beef stock or broth, fresh or commercial

Salt and freshly ground black pepper

THYME DUMPLINGS

2 teaspoons freshly chopped thyme

½ teaspoon freshly ground black pepper

1¼ cups commercial or homemade self-rising flour (page 17), divided

1 large egg

1 cup milk

To make the stew, heat the vegetable oil in a heavy Dutch oven. Add enough pieces of beef to the pan to cover the surface without touching. Cook on one side until deep brown. Turn and brown second side. Continue to turn each piece until they are brown on all sides. Remove and set aside. Brown any remaining pieces of beef if necessary.

When all beef is browned and removed from the pan, add the onion and cook a few minutes until slightly soft. Drain off all fat, return the beef to the pot with the onion, and add the potatoes, carrots, and beef stock. Bring to the boil, taste to see if the broth is salty enough, and season to taste with salt and pepper. Reduce heat, cover, and simmer 30 to 40 minutes until the potatoes are barely done. This may be done several hours in advance, cooled, and refrigerated. Cut any pieces of beef that are too large. Reheat to a simmer before adding dumplings. There should be enough broth to cover the meat.

To make the dumplings, mix the thyme and pepper with the flour, stirring it with a whisk or fork. Lightly fork-whisk the egg with the milk and add to the flour-thyme mixture. Stir to make a soft batter-like dough. Drop the dumplings into the still-simmering stew by tablespoons. Cover and simmer 10 minutes until the dumplings rise to the top and float. If the broth has reduced too much, the dumplings will need to be turned when nearly cooked to finish cooking the underside.

TIP: The stew may also be frozen. Thaw and reheat to a simmer before adding dumplings.

Chicken and Vegetables with Dumplings

Serves 6

There are two kinds of Southern dumplings. One uses drop biscuits (page 153). This one uses strips of dough. Either way, they are cooked in the flavorful broth during the final 10 minutes of cooking time so they will be tender and tasty. There is no reason why store-bought cooked chicken can't be used. Be careful, however, of salty commercial broth; add salt judiciously. If the soup is salty, add water if necessary before adding the biscuits.

CHICKEN AND VEGETABLES

3 cups shredded cooked chicken

4 to 5 cups chicken stock or broth, homemade or commercial

4 carrots, sliced 1-inch thick

1 medium onion, roughly chopped

2 celery stalks, sliced 1-inch thick

3 tablespoons butter

3 tablespoons all-purpose flour

¼ cup heavy cream or half-and-half (optional)

Salt and freshly ground black pepper

2 to 3 tablespoons chopped fresh parsley (optional)

Heat the broth to a boil in a saucepan. Add the carrots, onion, and celery; reduce the heat, cover, and simmer until just tender, about 10 to 15 minutes. Remove the vegetables with a slotted spoon and set broth and vegetables aside.

Heat the butter in a heavy Dutch oven or pot sufficient to hold the stew. When the butter is sizzling hot, stir in the flour all at once and continue stirring a few minutes over medium heat. It is alright if the flour browns slightly. Add 4 cups of the chicken broth and cream, if using, and bring to a boil. Season to taste with salt and pepper. Add the chicken and vegetables. Bring back to a boil and boil one minute to thoroughly reheat. (This may be made ahead, cooled, and refrigerated. Reheat the chicken, broth, and vegetables, and bring to the boil 15 to 20 minutes before adding dumplings.)

For the dumplings, fork-sift or whisk 2 cups of flour in a large bowl, preferably wider than it is deep, and set aside the remaining ¼ cup. Scatter the shortening over the flour and work in by rubbing fingers with the shortening and flour as if snapping thumb and fingers together (or use two forks or knives, or a pastry cutter) until the mixture looks like well-crumbled feta cheese, with no piece larger than a pea. Shake the bowl occasionally to allow the larger pieces of fat to bounce to the top of the flour, revealing the largest lumps that still need rubbing. If this method took longer than 5 minutes, place the bowl in the refrigerator for 5 minutes to rechill the fat.

Make a deep hollow in the center of the flour with the back of your hand. Pour the buttermilk into the hollow and stir with

DUMPLINGS

2¼ cups commercial or homemade self-rising flour (page 17)

¼ cup chilled shortening, roughly cut into ½-inch pieces

¾ cup buttermilk or milk

a rubber spatula or large metal spoon, using broad circular strokes to quickly pull the flour into the buttermilk. Mix just until the dry ingredients are moistened and the sticky dough begins to pull away from the sides of the bowl.

Lightly sprinkle a board or other clean surface with some of the reserved flour. Turn the dough out onto the board and sprinkle the top lightly with flour. With floured hands, fold the dough in half; roll dough out with a floured rolling pin into a ⅓- to ½-inch-thick round, using a little additional flour only if needed. Flour again if necessary and fold the dough in half a second time. Roll dough to ⅛- to ¼-inch-thick square. Use a pizza cutter or pastry wheel and cut the dough into 2-inch-long and ½-inch-wide strips. Separate from each other and set aside about 5 minutes. (These can be made ahead several hours and added dry to the broth if necessary. Avoid clumping the dumpling strips together.)

When the soup has returned to the boil, add the dumplings. Cover and boil 10 to 15 minutes, depending on the size of the dumplings, until the dumplings are cooked and firm. Add the parsley just before serving.

VARIATION: Add chopped parsley or freshly ground black pepper to taste to the dumpling dough.

*Overnight Biscuit, Sausage,
and Apple Casserole*

Tomorrow's Biscuits

While testing these recipes, we wound up with batches of biscuits we couldn't bear to throw away. Although we ate plenty along the way, we still had biscuits left over at the end of the day, and we just couldn't let them go. We began substituting biscuits in traditional recipes calling for sandwich and loaf bread, Italian and French bread, and just about every other kind of bread. We began with the obvious—mock soufflés called "Overnight Casseroles" (pages 165 and 166)—and then began branching out to discover the surprisingly good Biscuit Panzanella Salad (page 162) and remembering childhood's Breaded Tomatoes (page 160)—both immensely satisfying uses for leftover biscuits. So, while all the biscuit recipes in this book, by and large, can be cut in half, the lack of leftover biscuits could mean missing out on absolutely the best turkey dressing.

Breaded Tomatoes

Serves 4

After her grandmother passed, Cynthia's grandfather, Papa, said the dish he missed the most was his wife's breaded tomatoes. Cynthia baked it for him every time he came to visit.

3 cups torn or cut biscuits in ½-inch pieces

1 teaspoon granulated sugar

1 (14-ounce) can diced tomatoes

½ cup butter, melted

Preheat oven to 350 degrees F.

Grease a small casserole dish. Add crumbled biscuits and toss with sugar. Stir in the tomatoes. Drizzle the mixture with melted butter. Bake 30 to 35 minutes until the biscuit crumbs are light brown.

Tomato Biscuit Soup

Serves 4

Thick and warm, this soup will chase away any winter's chill. It's also delicious in the summer made with fresh tomatoes from the garden.

3 tablespoons extra-virgin olive oil, plus extra for brushing the biscuits

1 yellow onion, chopped

3 cloves garlic, minced

2 (28-ounce) cans whole tomatoes

¼ cup finely shredded and packed fresh basil leaves, divided

¼ teaspoon granulated sugar

¼ teaspoon red pepper flakes

Salt and freshly ground black pepper

2 cups torn or cut biscuits in ½-inch pieces

6 cups chicken stock or broth (fresh or commercial), heated

4 biscuits

Parmesan cheese

Heat the olive oil in a large pot; add the onion and sauté until translucent. Add the garlic, tomatoes, half of the basil, sugar, red pepper flakes, salt, and pepper to the pot, stirring to combine. Bring to a simmer; cook for 8 minutes until the tomatoes have softened. Add the biscuit pieces and the chicken stock. Simmer for 15 minutes more.

Preheat oven to 350 degrees F.

Brush the 4 biscuits with olive oil and sprinkle with Parmesan cheese. Bake until the cheese has melted and the biscuits are warm and toasty.

Divide the soup between four bowls. Sprinkle with reserved basil and top each bowl with the toasted cheese biscuit.

VARIATION: Substitute 8 medium chopped fresh tomatoes for the canned.

Biscuit Panzanella Salad

Serves 6 to 8

When we had some leftover biscuits one day, we toasted them and tossed them into a salad. The toasted biscuits enhanced the flavor of the already delicious salad, and their structure was perfect for the salad. It is best to enjoy this salad the day that is it tossed with the dressing; leftovers are not as enjoyable.

4½ cups torn or cut biscuits in 2-inch pieces

1½ tablespoons olive oil

4 medium tomatoes, roughly chopped

1 small onion, sliced thinly

2 tablespoons chopped fresh basil

2 tablespoons chopped fresh lemon balm

2 to 3 tablespoons lemon juice, or to taste

Preheat oven to 400 degrees F.

Sprinkle the biscuit pieces with olive oil and toss lightly in a large bowl. Move the biscuit pieces to a baking sheet and toast in a preheated oven for 15 minutes or until tinged with brown. Remove biscuits from oven and toss in a large serving bowl with olive oil, tomatoes, onion, basil, lemon balm, and lemon juice.

Sausage, Fennel, and Apple or Pear Dressing or Stuffing

Serves 6 to 8

Sausage and apple are naturally good together; mixed with biscuit crumbs they make a wonderful, flavorful, near-healthy dressing. A real plus is turkey stock. I make mine ahead of time, using browned turkey wings, but turkey stock is also available now in the average grocery store.

½ cup butter, divided

½ pound sweet Italian pork or turkey sausage

1 large onion, chopped

3 garlic cloves, chopped

1 to 2 fennel bulbs, finely chopped

1 to 2 red or other cooking apple or pear

¼ cup apple juice

1 cup chopped pecans

1 to 2 cups turkey or chicken stock or broth (fresh or commercial), divided

4 cups torn or cut biscuits or bread in ½-inch pieces

3 tablespoons chopped fresh thyme, marjoram, and/or oregano, divided

1 tablespoon fennel frond

Preheat oven to 350 degrees F.

Melt several tablespoons of butter in a large skillet. Crumble the sausage and add to the hot pan. Brown, remove from pan with a slotted spoon, and set aside. Add the onion and cook until soft. Add the garlic and fennel. Chop one apple or pear, leaving skin on; add to the pan and cook a few minutes until the fennel and apple are slightly soft. Add the rest of the butter in pieces, making sure it melts. Cool slightly. Return the sausage, apple juice, pecans, 1 cup of stock, biscuits or bread, and half the herbs; toss everything together until the bread is well moistened, adding stock if needed. Set aside the other apple or pear, the remaining herbs, and the remaining stock.

Move the mixture to an 11 x 13-inch baking dish and bake 20 to 30 minutes until the bread is lightly browned. Serve hot. Or cool, wrap, and freeze, then defrost in microwave or refrigerator and reheat in a 350 degree oven for 20 minutes. Add the remaining apple and herbs, pushing the apple or pear in for color. Add any stock as needed.

Overnight Biscuit Cheese Casserole

Serves 6 to 8

The South is a land of church dinners and suppers, where toting food is an honored tradition. So is fixing food ahead of time to be heated or cooked later. I have known people as well as restaurants to pass this off as a soufflé—and why not? It is amazingly light and fluffy. Dijon mustard brings out the flavor of mild cheeses. A strong sharp cheddar or blue cheese will not need the full amount, but a Gruyere or Swiss cheese will. Feel free to experiment. I have frozen the casserole after baking with good success, and have baked and refrigerated it up to three days, and then reheated it with the same results.

6 tablespoons butter

3 cups torn or cut biscuits in ½-inch pieces

9 large eggs, beaten

4 cups grated sharp cheddar or other cheese (Swiss, Gruyere, blue)

1½ to 2 tablespoons Dijon mustard

Dash of ground red cayenne pepper (optional)

3 cups milk

Salt and freshly ground black pepper

Melt the butter in a large skillet over medium heat and stir in the biscuit to coat with the butter. Remove from the heat and let stand for 5 minutes until the butter is absorbed. Place the biscuit pieces in a large resealable plastic bag.

Whisk together the eggs, cheese, mustard, red pepper, and milk in a large bowl, season to taste with salt and pepper, and then transfer the mixture to the plastic bag. Place the bag inside another resealable plastic bag with the zipper facing another direction in order to prevent leaks. Refrigerate at least 2 hours, preferably overnight or up to two days.

When ready to bake, preheat oven to 350 degrees F. Pour mixture into a buttered 13 x 9 x 2-inch baking dish or divide between two 1½-quart casseroles. Bake covered 30 minutes. Uncover and bake another 30 minutes until eggs are set and the center measures 200 degrees F on an instant-read thermometer.

Note: This recipe may be scaled up or down. For each additional biscuit, add another egg, 2 teaspoons of butter, a little more than 1 ounce of cheese, ½ teaspoon mustard, and ⅓ cup of milk.

VARIATION: Add 2 tablespoons chopped fresh herbs.

VARIATION: Substituting Buttermilk Raisin Cinnamon Pecan Biscuits (page 114), a little sugar, and removing the cheese makes a lovely variation for a brunch, very different from a bread pudding.

Overnight Biscuit, Sausage, and Apple Casserole

Serves 8

Sausage and apple is one of my favorite food combinations, and I find ways to cook it into everything from quiches to this soufflé-like casserole, great for a brunch or long weekend.

2 pounds bulk sausage

2 tart apples, cored and sliced

6 cups torn or cut biscuits in ½-inch pieces

9 eggs, beaten

¾ teaspoon Dijon mustard

1½ cups grated sharp cheddar cheese

3 cups milk

Salt and freshly ground black pepper

Fry the sausage in a skillet, breaking it up as it cooks, and drain on a paper towel. Reserve the fat and let the sausage cool. Sauté the apples in the reserved fat, remove from pan, and let cool.

Move the biscuit pieces to a large resealable plastic bag.

Whisk together the eggs, mustard, cheese, and milk in a large bowl. Stir in the sausage and apples. Season to taste with salt and pepper. Transfer the mixture to the plastic bag. Place the bag inside another resealable plastic bag with the zipper facing another direction in order to prevent leaks. Refrigerate at least 2 hours, preferably overnight or up to 2 days.

When ready to bake, preheat oven to 350 degrees F. Pour mixture into a buttered 13 x 9 x 2-inch baking dish or divide between two 1½-quart casseroles. Bake covered 30 minutes. Uncover and bake another 30 minutes until eggs are set and the center measures 200 degrees F on an instant-read thermometer.

VARIATION: Substitute Sweet Potato Biscuits (page 120) for the regular ones here, especially in the autumn.

gilding the Lily

Biscuits accept almost any jam, jelly, spread, or filling between their fluffy layers. From the tart Hot Pepper Jelly (page 176) to the sweet Fig Jam Filling (page 173), there is a butter, spread, topping, or filling for every occasion, mood, and taste.

Citrus Butter

Makes ½ cup

This butter completely changes a biscuit, making it sweet and snappy.

½ cup butter, room temperature

1 tablespoon confectioners' sugar

1 teaspoon finely grated orange or lemon rind, no white attached

Combine all ingredients and serve right away, or move to small ramekins or small decorative pots and refrigerate or freeze. To serve slices or pats, shape butter into a roll in plastic wrap or waxed paper and refrigerate or freeze. Slice and put onto plates as butter pats, or slip a slice into or on top of a biscuit.

Herb Butter

Makes ½ cup

This was the butter I served at my restaurant in Social Circle, Georgia, night after night.

½ cup butter, room temperature

½ teaspoon each freshly chopped thyme and marjoram, or 1 teaspoon basil

Combine all ingredients and serve right away, or move to small ramekins or small decorative pots and refrigerate or freeze. To serve slices or pats, shape butter into a roll in plastic wrap or waxed paper and refrigerate or freeze. Slice and put onto plates as butter pats, or slip a slice into or on top of a biscuit.

Norman's Compound Butter

Makes ½ cup

Cynthia's son, Norman, developed a passion for cooking while in college and has a cook's instinct for complementary flavors. His compound butter plays equally well with traditional biscuits as it does with cornmeal biscuits.

½ cup butter, softened

2 tablespoons chopped fresh cilantro

Juice of ½ lime

Grated rind of ½ lime, no white attached

Combine all ingredients and serve right away, or move to small ramekins or small decorative pots and refrigerate or freeze. To serve slices or pats, shape butter into a roll in plastic wrap or waxed paper and refrigerate or freeze. Slice and put onto plates as butter pats, or slip a slice into or on top of a biscuit.

Nut Butter

Makes 1 cup

Try this for a ladies' tea, especially when gentlemen are included.

¼ cup butter, room temperature

½ cup finely chopped almonds or walnuts

¼ cup apricot or peach preserves

Combine all ingredients and serve right away, or move to small ramekins or small decorative pots and refrigerate or freeze. To serve slices or pats, shape butter into a roll in plastic wrap or waxed paper and refrigerate or freeze. Slice and put onto plates as butter pats, or slip a slice into or on top of a biscuit.

Orange-Honey Butter

Makes ½ cup

This make-ahead butter is delicious served with split biscuits or pancakes. Or anything.

½ cup butter, softened

1 teaspoon grated orange rind, no white attached

2 tablespoons honey

Combine all ingredients and serve right away, or move to small ramekins or small decorative pots and refrigerate or freeze. To serve slices or pats, shape butter into a roll in plastic wrap or waxed paper and refrigerate or freeze. Slice and put onto plates as butter pats, or slip a slice into or on top of a biscuit.

Honey Mustard Sauce

Makes ⅓ cup

This is terrific with sliced ham, cheese, and chicken inside split biscuits.

⅓ cup mayonnaise

3 tablespoons whole-grain or Dijon mustard

2 tablespoons honey

1 tablespoon grated orange rind, no white included

Whisk together all ingredients. Use right away or cover and refrigerate as necessary.

Orange glaze

Makes 1 cup

This is a traditional glaze for biscuits, scones, and cakes.

¾ cup confectioners' sugar

1 teaspoon grated orange rind, no white attached

3 to 4 teaspoons orange juice

Mix the sugar, grated orange rind, and enough orange juice to reach brushing consistency. Brush on top of hot biscuits or scones.

Fig Jam Filling

Makes 1 cup

For those of us who love figs, this is better than any other jam. Not, of course that we don't love all jams.

½ cup dried figs

Boiling water

½ cup hot water

2 tablespoons granulated sugar

2 teaspoons lemon juice

Cover figs with boiling water and let stand 5 to 10 minutes. Drain, snip off stems, and cut fine using scissors. Move the figs to a heavy-bottomed saucepan with the hot water and sugar. Cook gently, stirring constantly, until the consistency of jam. Stir in lemon juice. Let cool.

Easy Refrigerator Strawberry Jam

Makes 4 cups

This recipe doesn't require any pectin, making it easy to throw together without another trip to the store. I don't have a good storage place for jams and jellies, as my pantry is very small; therefore, I prefer a refrigerator jam.

2 pounds fresh strawberries, hulled

4 cups granulated sugar

2 tablespoons lemon juice

2 tablespoons orange juice

Limoncello liqueur to taste (optional)

To test the jam's readiness after cooking, move a small plate to the freezer until needed.

Crush the strawberries in batches to make 4 cups of mashed berries. Move the mashed berries to a heavy pan and stir in the sugar, lemon juice, and orange juice over low heat until the sugar is dissolved. Add Limoncello if desired. Increase the heat to high, and bring the mixture to the boil. Boil, stirring often, until the mixture reaches 220 degrees F on an instant-read or candy thermometer.

Remove the plate from the freezer and drop a teaspoon of the jam onto the plate. Return the plate to the freezer for 1 minute. Remove the plate and make a line with your finger through the jam on the plate. If the jam doesn't run together, it is ready. Pour into clean containers and keep refrigerated.

VARIATION: To can, transfer the jam to hot sterile jars, leaving ¼ to ½ inch headspace, and seal.

Lemon Curd (Lemon Cheese)

Makes 2½ cups

This recipe emerges in old and modern French, English, and Southern recipes. Thomas Jefferson and Martha Washington's recipe collections show its use as well. The curd itself is delicious as a filling for cakes, meringues, and tarts.

Like mayonnaise, it will last a long time in the refrigerator as it has a high degree of acid (a low pH). Once it is mixed with something that changes the acidity, it will not last as long. Since acidity of citrus varies, and the home cook has no real idea of its strength, some care should be taken. Usually it may be kept up to a month, tightly sealed, in the refrigerator.

Note: Peculiarly, egg yolks do not like sugar sitting on top of them without any agitation from spoon or whisk. The sugar tends to "cook" the egg yolk.

5 large egg yolks

1 cup granulated sugar

1/2 cup unsalted butter, softened

3 to 4 lemons to make ½ cup lemon juice

3 tablespoons (approximately) grated lemon rind

Lightly whisk the egg yolks in a heavy saucepan, or use a bain-marie or double boiler. Whisk in the sugar and butter, then the lemon juice. Set the rind aside.

Stir the egg mixture with a rubber spatula over low heat for 5 to 10 minutes until thick but still falling easily from a spoon, making sure to scrape the sides and bottom occasionally. The temperature should register approximately 180 to 190 degrees F on a thermometer, but it is not a disaster if the mixture simmers at the edges of the pan. Quickly strain.

It should be smooth with no egg bits remaining.* Add the rind. Taste for flavor and add more juice or rind if necessary and available. Remove from the heat and cool. Store in the refrigerator in a tightly covered jar.

*Note: If egg bits remain, don't throw away the curd. It still tastes wonderful as a spread for family biscuits.

VARIATION: To lighten, fold in whipped cream, mascarpone, or meringue.

VARIATION: Lime, orange, and other citrus juices as well as cooked pineapple are delicious variations. Adjust the amount of juice as needed, keeping in mind acid is necessary for thickening the mixture and lowering the pH.

Hot Pepper Jelly

Makes about 8 cups

*Pepper jelly can be made with any kind of
pepper, some even use bell peppers, which
produce a non-hot version. Bell peppers hardly
fit the bill for a region where homemade hot
sauce made from hot peppers and vinegar used
to sit on every kitchen table for sprinkling on
food during the meal. The pepper jelly I first
made was from a pepper shaped much like a
horn; it was called a "cow horn pepper" even
though it was a misnomer. Three or four times
the size of a Tabasco or jalapeño pepper, it made
a hot but still mild jelly. Now the market is
flooded with pepper jellies made from every kind
of pepper, including the feisty Scotch Bonnet,
some of which are a bit too hot for me.*

1 cup seeded and coarsely chopped hot
peppers (red, green, and/or yellow)

1 cup chopped onion

1½ cups apple cider vinegar

5 cups sugar

1 (3-ounce) pouch liquid pectin

Combine the hot peppers, onion, and vinegar in a food
processor or blender until the peppers and onion are very finely
chopped. Add to the sugar in a heavy nonaluminum pot. Bring
to the boil and boil for 1 minute; remove from the heat and stir
in the pectin. Return to the heat, bring to the boil, and boil 1
minute longer. Let the jelly sit for 5 minutes before skimming
off any foam with a slotted spoon. Ladle into sterilized jars
and seal. Turn the jars upside down occasionally to keep the
peppers mixed until the jelly is cool and set.

As a general rule, the smaller the pepper, the hotter it
is, with the exception perhaps of the Spanish padrone
pepper or its cousin the shishito pepper.

The hottest part of a pepper is the seed, which sits
inside next to the interior of the skin where it first
transfers its hotness. It is important to remove the
seeds judiciously, using plastic gloves or bags to protect
the hands and the eyes and mouth in particular from
the residual heat. When seeding a small quantity, slide
the tip of a peeler right up the halved pepper, removing
seeds and part of the interior. A larger quantity goes
faster by pushing the finger up the middle. Keep the
peppers covered while working in batches to keep the
air free of the burning aromas. Once the pepper jelly is
finished, the pain is forgotten.

Sausage-Bacon Gravy

Makes 3½ cups

Southerners dream about sausage-bacon gravy ladled on their biscuits, just like their grandmothers on the farm cooked. This is hearty enough for a Sunday supper, a late Saturday brunch, or a farmhand before a hard day's labor, which is the reason it was originally served. It does seem like gilding the lily to use both bacon and sausage in this gravy—so omit one or the other if desired.

8 slices bacon

4 sausage patties

⅓ cup all-purpose flour

3½ cups milk

Salt and freshly ground black pepper

Fry the bacon and the patties together in a large, heavy frying pan or iron skillet. When the bacon and/or sausage are crispy, remove and drain on paper towels as needed.

Stir the flour into the remaining fat and continue to stir a minute or two over heat until it is slightly browned. Stir in the milk and continue to stir until it thickens, 5 to 10 minutes depending on the size of the frying pan. Season to taste with salt and pepper, remembering the meat has salt and pepper in it already.

Dumpling Gravy

This should only be done with the best of stocks and gravies, I'm afraid; but once done right, it is one of the most memorable things you've ever done with leftover Thanksgiving turkey stock or gravy.

GRAVY

4 cups turkey or chicken stock,
or dilute gravy to 4 cups

1 cup butter

Salt and freshly ground black pepper

DUMPLINGS

1 cup Homemade Refrigerator Biscuit Mix
(page 50) mixed with ⅔ cup milk

TO FINISH

1 cup milk

Bring stock to the boil in a large heavy pot. Add butter and season to taste with salt and pepper.

Meanwhile, prepare the dumpling or biscuit dough. Drop the dumplings by rounded tablespoons into boiling stock. Reduce heat to simmer, cover, and cook about five minutes, turning dumplings as needed, until they have swelled up through the stock and are puffy and cooked through. Stir in the milk. Bring back to the boil and serve hot. Go to bed with teddy bear.

Chocolate Gravy

Makes 1 cup

Chocolate was always cheaper in the colonies than in Europe, where there were high taxes and shipping fees. For that reason, soldiers in the early wars were given chocolate as part of their rations since coffee was scarce. No doubt that chocolate gravy was derived from their cooking and is the reason it is still made in some places today.

¼ cup butter

¼ cup cocoa

¼ cup granulated sugar

¼ cup milk or water

Stir all ingredients together in a small heavy pot over medium heat. Continue stirring until the ingredients are melted together. Turn up the heat slightly, bring to a simmer, and carefully simmer until the sauce becomes the thickness of gravy. Serve hot with biscuits.

Butterscotch Sauce

Makes 1 cup

The apple cider vinegar adds a bite to the sauce, which is needed to take it to the next level for flavor.

½ cup butter

1 cup light or dark brown sugar

1 cup heavy cream

1 teaspoon vanilla extract

2 teaspoons apple cider vinegar

½ teaspoon salt

Melt the butter and sugar together in a heavy-bottomed saucepan or an enameled cast-iron pot over medium heat and cook until the sugar has melted completely and the mixture has taken on a thick frothy appearance, "lava-like." Remove the pot from the heat and whisk in the cream until thoroughly incorporated. Let cool for 10 minutes; add the vanilla extract, vinegar, and salt.

Caramel Sauce

Makes 2 cups

Caramel sauce is versatile and delicious. Follow these instructions carefully as the boiled sugar syrup is extremely hot. The corn syrup in this recipe acts as a stabilizer. The trick is to dissolve the sugar before bringing it to a boil. This is doubly important when it is humid and the sugar is clumping and retaining moisture.

If the syrup boils before the sugar is dissolved, crystallization will occur. The same thing will happen if, once the sugar is dissolved and begins to boil, a spoon, the sides of the pan, or other objects with grains of sugar attached cause un-dissolved sugar to drop into the boiling liquid. For this reason, some like to cover the pan, letting the resulting steam wash down the sides.

Because covering the pan can cause inattention, I prefer a cup of water and a pastry brush. I brush down the sides of the pan with the wet pastry brush before bringing to the boil, and I return the spoon to the cup of water in between stirring. A different result comes from the different kinds of sugars, with preferences open to the cook.

1 cup granulated sugar, or a mixture of brown and granulated sugar, or brown sugar, or honey

¼ cup white corn syrup

2 cups water, divided

Heat the sugar in a saucepan with the corn syrup and 1 cup water, but do not boil. Stir to completely dissolve the sugar in the water if necessary. Brush down the sides of the pan with some water if there are sugar crystals on its side.

Add cold water to a frying or roasting pan large enough to immerse the caramel pan if the caramel browns too quickly.

Once the sugar is completely dissolved, bring up to the boil. Boil steadily until large bubbles form on the surface. Watch closely as the caramel turns from bursting bubbles to little bubbles and then to caramel. Cover your hand or use an oven mitt and tip the pan once it colors, so the sugar is uniformly colored. When it turns amber, remove from the heat. It will continue to bubble. If it becomes as dark as mahogany, move it to the pan of water carefully to cool it down immediately and stop the cooking. (Be careful of the bubbling water and sugar.)

Wipe the bottom of the pan if necessary and return to the heat, adding the remaining cup of water. Return to the boil. If part of the caramel syrup has solidified, stir with a clean wooden spoon so the caramel will be evenly distributed. Bring back to the boil, and boil until reduced by ¼ and slightly syrupy. Cool, pour into another container, and chill. This will last several weeks in the refrigerator, covered.

VARIATION: Add heavy whipping cream in place of 1 cup of water. It will boil up, but not over, in a large enough pan. It makes a much richer, creamier sauce.

Hayley Daen's Cranberry Buttermilk Scones

Desserts

Biscuits appeared in the breadbasket on our supper table with regularity but with a dual purpose. The first biscuit or two were eaten with butter and usually sopped up gravy or helped push errant peas onto a spoon or fork. The remaining became dessert, slathered with honey. Memories of lingering at the dinner table, just the girls, with the biscuits, butter, and honey, are among Cynthia's fondest memories of spending time at the table with her mother.

Stepping up the culinary ladder from a simple biscuit, one can enjoy shortcakes, scones, and cobblers. Berry-Biscuit Summer Pudding (page 204) and Biscuit Trifle (page 203) are fuss-free and are best made from day-old biscuits. Biscuit bread puddings epitomize the warmth of a homemade dessert, and the Cinnamon-Raisin (page 208) or Ginger-Banana (page 207) versions here will end any meal with a sigh. Lazy Girl Peach Cobbler (page 200) is a staple in our homes; it's more than a desperation dessert—it's one of those things we cook because it makes people happy—whether eaten by four or forty.

Biscuit dough is also versatile, as demonstrated by our Fig Roll Loaf (page 196), Peach Pinwheels (page 194), and Fried Pies (page 198).

White Lily Sweet Cake Biscuits

Makes 8 to 10

A shortcake is a sweeter biscuit and a shortbread is a denser cookie-type dough. A sweet cake is more like a cake, probably due to the egg but also because of the whipped cream.

2¼ cups commercial or homemade
self-rising flour (page 17), divided

¼ cup granulated sugar

¼ cup chilled butter, roughly
cut into ¼-inch pieces
AND
¼ cup chilled butter, roughly
cut into ½-inch pieces

1 large egg

⅔ cup heavy cream, divided

3 cups sliced strawberries or whole
raspberries, sweetened with ¼ cup sugar

1 cup blueberries (optional)

1 cup heavy cream, whipped

Softened butter, for brushing

Preheat oven to 425 degrees F.

Select the baking pan by determining if a soft or crisp exterior is desired. For a soft exterior, use an 8- or 9-inch cake pan, pizza pan, or ovenproof skillet where the biscuits will nestle together snugly, creating the soft exterior while baking. For a crisp exterior, select a baking sheet or other baking pan where the biscuits can be placed wider apart, allowing air to circulate and creating a crisper exterior, and brush the pan with butter.

Fork-sift or whisk 2 cups of flour and sugar in a large bowl, preferably wider than it is deep, and set aside the remaining ¼ cup of flour. Scatter the ¼-inch-size pieces of chilled fat over the flour and work in by rubbing fingers with the fat and flour as if snapping thumb and fingers together (or use two forks or knives, or a pastry cutter) until the mixture looks like well-crumbled feta cheese. Scatter the ½-inch-size pieces of chilled fat over the flour mixture and continue snapping thumb and fingers together until no pieces remain larger than a pea. Shake the bowl occasionally to allow the larger pieces of fat to bounce to the top of the flour, revealing the largest lumps that still need rubbing. If this method took longer than 5 minutes, place the bowl in the refrigerator for 5 minutes to rechill the fat.

Make a deep hollow in the center of the flour with the back of your hand. Lightly beat together the egg and ⅓ cup of the cream, and pour the mixture into the hollow, reserving the remaining ⅓ cup of the cream. Stir the mixture with a rubber spatula or large metal spoon, using broad circular strokes

to quickly pull the flour into the liquid. Mix just until the dry ingredients are moistened and the sticky dough begins to pull away from the sides of the bowl. If there is some flour remaining on the bottom and sides of the bowl, stir in 1 to 4 tablespoons of reserved cream, just enough to incorporate the remaining flour into the shaggy wettish dough. If the dough is too wet, use more flour when shaping.

Lightly sprinkle a board or other clean surface with some of the reserved flour. Turn the dough out onto the board and sprinkle the top lightly with flour. With floured hands, fold the dough in half, and pat dough out into a ⅓- to ½-inch-thick round, using a little additional flour only if needed. Flour again if necessary, and fold the dough in half a second time. If the dough is still clumpy, pat and fold a third time. Pat dough out into a ½-inch-thick round for a normal biscuit, ¾-inch-thick for a tall biscuit, and 1-inch-thick for a giant biscuit. Brush off any visible flour from the top. For each biscuit, dip a 2-inch biscuit cutter into the reserved flour and cut out the biscuits, starting at the outside edge and cutting very close together, being careful not to twist the cutter. The scraps may be combined to make additional biscuits, although these scraps make tougher biscuits. For hand-shaping and other variations, see pages 24–26.

Using a metal spatula if necessary, move the biscuits to the pan or baking sheet. Brush tops lightly with some of the reserved cream. Bake the biscuits on the top rack of the oven for a total of 12 to 15 minutes, depending on thickness, until light golden brown. After 6 minutes, rotate the pan in the oven so that the front of the pan is now turned to the back, and check to see if the bottoms are browning too quickly. If so, slide another baking pan underneath to add insulation and retard browning. Continue baking another 6 to 9 minutes until the biscuits are light golden brown. When the biscuits are done, remove from the oven and lightly brush the tops with softened or melted butter. Turn the biscuits out upside down on a plate to cool slightly.

Toss berries together. Split biscuits in half and spoon fruit between layers. Replace top layer and spoon on additional fruit. Add whipped cream on top. Garnish with fresh whole fruit.

Hayley Daen's Cranberry Buttermilk Scones

Makes 12 scones

It is difficult to find something more pleasant than a beautiful flaky scone accompanied by a steamy cup of tea on a rainy afternoon. With their subtle sweetness and ethereal layers, these scones are as addicting as they come. The cranberries are tart and chewy, and the lemon zest adds a little brightness that highlights the tang of the buttermilk, all working together to create a marvelous scone. Hayley Daen is a whiz at scones—with or without eggs. She makes them at home regularly and frequently brought them in when she interned with me one summer.

4 ¾ cups all-purpose flour, divided

1 tablespoon baking powder

¼ teaspoon baking soda

½ cup granulated sugar

1¼ teaspoons salt

1 cup chilled butter, roughly cut into ½-inch pieces

1¾ cups buttermilk, divided

Grated rind of 1 lemon, no white attached

½ cup dried cranberries

3 tablespoons melted butter

Turbinado sugar for sprinkling

Preheat oven to 400 degrees F.

Fork-sift or whisk 4 ½ cups of flour, baking powder, baking soda, sugar, and salt in a large bowl, preferably wider than deep, and set aside the remaining ¼ cup of flour. Scatter the butter over the flour and work in by rubbing fingers with the butter and flour as if snapping thumb and fingers together (or use two forks or knives, or a pastry cutter) until the mixture is in thin sheets that resemble Frosted Flakes cereal. Shake the bowl occasionally to allow the larger pieces of fat to bounce to the top of the flour, revealing the largest lumps that still need rubbing. If this method took longer than 5 minutes, place the bowl in the refrigerator for 5 minutes to rechill the fat.

Make a deep hollow in the center of the flour with the back of your hand. Pour 1½ cups of buttermilk into the hollow, reserving ¼ cup, and sprinkle in the grated lemon rind. Stir the buttermilk and rind with a rubber spatula or large metal spoon, using broad circular strokes to quickly pull the flour into the buttermilk. Mix just until the dry ingredients are moistened and the sticky dough begins to pull away from the sides of the bowl. If there is some flour remaining on the bottom and sides of the bowl, stir in 1 to 4 tablespoons of reserved buttermilk, just enough to incorporate the remaining flour into the dough, which will be a bit dry and crumbly. Fold in the cranberries.

Lightly sprinkle a board or other clean surface with some of the reserved flour. Turn the dough out onto the floured surface. With floured hands, pat dough into a 5 x 18-inch

rectangle about 1 inch thick. (The dough will be very shaggy and will seem as if it could not possibly stay together; do not fret or try to make it into a smooth, cohesive dough. The lumpiness will help make a flakier, more split-able scone in the long run.) Cut dough into 12 triangles, brush each with melted butter, and sprinkle with turbinado sugar.

Using a metal spatula if necessary, move the scones to a baking sheet lined with parchment paper. Bake the scones for 25 minutes or until the scones are golden brown and firm to the touch. Remove from oven and serve warm, or rest on a wire rack to cool.

Cut the dough into triangles.

Hayley Daen's Brown Sugar Shortcakes

Makes 12 shortcakes

Is there a more fitting end to a refreshing summer meal than shortcake? If there is, I have yet to find it. Layered with sweetened whipped cream and berries fresh from the farm stand, these shortcakes are truly incredible. The sugar caramelizes on the bottom of the skillet, leaving a crisp exterior that is surprisingly fun to eat. Hayley uses turbinado sugar, which is not available in all markets. We have used brown sugar here.

2½ cups all-purpose flour, divided

⅓ cup packed light or dark brown sugar

2 teaspoons baking powder

¼ teaspoon baking soda

½ teaspoon salt

⅓ cup chilled butter, roughly cut into ½-inch pieces

1¼ cups buttermilk, divided

1 tablespoon light or brown sugar

Preheat oven to 425 degrees F.

Fork-sift or whisk 2¼ cups of flour, brown sugar, baking powder, baking soda, and salt in a large bowl, preferably wider than it is deep, and set aside the remaining ¼ cup of flour. Scatter the butter over the flour and work in by rubbing fingers with the butter and flour as if snapping thumb and fingers together (or use two forks or knives, or a pastry cutter) until the mixture looks like well-crumbled feta cheese, with no piece larger than a pea. Shake the bowl occasionally to allow the larger pieces of fat to bounce to the top of the flour, revealing the largest lumps that still need rubbing. If this method took longer than 5 minutes, place the bowl in the refrigerator for 5 minutes to rechill the fat.

Make a deep hollow in the center of the flour with the back of your hand. Pour 1 cup of buttermilk into the hollow, reserving ¼ cup, and stir with a rubber spatula or large metal spoon, using broad circular strokes to quickly pull the flour into the buttermilk. Mix just until the dry ingredients are moistened and the sticky dough begins to pull away from the sides of the bowl. If there is some flour remaining on the bottom and sides of the bowl, stir in 1 to 4 tablespoons of reserved milk, just enough to incorporate the remaining flour into the shaggy wettish dough. If the dough is too wet, use more flour when shaping.

Scrape the dough out into two 6-inch skillets. Sprinkle the top with light or brown sugar. Bake the biscuits on the top rack of the oven for a total of 10 to 14 minutes, depending on thickness, until light golden brown. After 6 minutes, rotate the pan in the oven so that the front of the pan is now turned to the back. Continue baking another 4 to 8 minutes until the biscuits are light golden brown. When the biscuits are done, remove from the oven and cut into 6 triangles. Serve hot, split in half and filled with desired accompaniments.

VARIATIONS: Sprinkle with confectioners' sugar; split and fill with whipped cream and peaches, berries, mangos, or other fruit; or split and fill with raspberry jam or Nutella.

Caramel Bread Sticks

Makes 12 dozen sticks

Like Chocolate Soldiers (page 210), this appeals to the child in all of us who wants to sit at the table with something tasty to be dunked.

4 ¾ cups all-purpose flour, divided

1 teaspoon salt

1 cup light or dark brown sugar

¼ cup chilled shortening, roughly cut into ¼-inch pieces
AND
¼ cup chilled shortening, roughly cut into ½-inch pieces

1 ¼ cups milk, divided

Ground nutmeg

Ground cinnamon

Preheat oven to 350 degrees F.

Fork-sift or whisk 4 ½ cups of flour, salt, and brown sugar in a large bowl, preferably wider than it is deep, and set aside the remaining ¼ cup of flour. Scatter the ¼-inch-size pieces of chilled fat over the flour and work in by rubbing fingers with the fat and flour as if snapping thumb and fingers together (or use two forks or knives, or a pastry cutter) until the mixture looks like well-crumbled feta cheese. Scatter the ½-inch-size pieces of chilled fat over the flour mixture and continue snapping thumb and fingers together until no pieces remain larger than a pea. Shake the bowl occasionally to allow the larger pieces of fat to bounce to the top of the flour, revealing the largest lumps that still need rubbing. If this method took longer than 5 minutes, place the bowl in the refrigerator for 5 minutes to rechill the fat.

Make a deep hollow in the center of the flour with the back of your hand. Pour 1 cup of milk into the hollow, reserving ¼ cup, and stir with a rubber spatula or large metal spoon, using broad circular strokes to quickly pull the flour into the milk. Mix just until the dry ingredients are moistened and the sticky dough begins to pull away from the sides of the bowl. If there is some flour remaining on the bottom and sides of the bowl, stir in 1 to 4 tablespoons of reserved milk, just enough to incorporate the remaining flour into the stiff dough.

Lightly sprinkle a board or other clean surface with some of the reserved flour. Turn the dough out onto the board and sprinkle the top lightly with flour. With floured hands, fold the dough in half, and roll dough out with a floured rolling pin into a ⅓- to ½-inch-thick round, using a little additional flour only if needed. Flour again if necessary and fold the dough in half a second time. Roll dough out to ⅛-inch thickness. Brush off any visible flour from the top. Cut dough into 1 x 3-inch strips using a pastry wheel, pizza cutter, or knife.

Using a metal spatula if necessary, move the strips to an ungreased baking sheet and sprinkle with nutmeg and cinnamon. Bake the strips on the top rack of the oven for a total of 15 to 20 minutes. After 10 minutes, rotate the pan in the oven so that the front of the pan is now turned to the back. Continue baking another 5 to 10 minutes until crisp and golden brown.

Peach Pinwheels

Makes 8

Yum, yum, yum. I am a peach devotee. This is ideal for clingstone peaches, which come early in the season and are easier to cook with. I've also made this with frozen peaches.

2¼ cups all-purpose flour, divided

3 teaspoons baking powder

1 teaspoon salt

4 tablespoons chilled shortening, roughly cut into ½-inch pieces

¾ cup milk, divided

1 cup chopped peaches

1 cup light or dark brown sugar

½ cup water

1 tablespoon butter

Preheat oven to 375 degrees F.

Fork-sift or whisk 2 cups of flour with baking powder and salt in a large bowl, preferably wider than it is deep, and set aside the remaining ¼ cup of flour. Scatter the shortening over the flour and work in by rubbing fingers with the shortening and flour as if snapping thumb and fingers together (or use two forks or knives, or a pastry cutter) until the mixture looks like well-crumbled feta cheese, with no piece larger than a pea. Shake the bowl occasionally to allow the larger pieces of fat to bounce to the top of the flour, revealing the largest lumps that still need rubbing. If this method took longer than 5 minutes, place the bowl in the refrigerator for 5 minutes to rechill the fat.

Make a deep hollow in the center of the flour with the back of your hand. Pour ½ cup of milk into the hollow, reserving ¼ cup, and stir with a rubber spatula or large metal spoon, using broad circular strokes to quickly pull the flour into the liquid. Mix just until the dry ingredients are moistened and the sticky dough begins to pull away from the sides of the bowl. If there is some flour remaining on the bottom and sides of the bowl, stir in 1 to 4 tablespoons of reserved milk, just enough to incorporate the remaining flour into the shaggy wettish dough. If the dough is too wet, use more flour when shaping.

Lightly sprinkle a board or other clean surface with some of the reserved flour. Turn the dough out onto the board and sprinkle the top lightly with flour. With floured hands, fold the dough in half, and pat dough out into a ⅓- to ½-inch-thick round, using a little additional flour only if needed. Flour again if necessary and fold the dough in half a second time. Pat dough out into a ¼-inch-thick rectangle, using a little additional flour if necessary to keep the dough from sticking to the surface.

Sprinkle with chopped peaches. Roll the dough jelly-roll style using the heel of one hand and starting from the longest side. Cut across the roll into 8 slices and move to a 9 x 13-inch baking dish, cut side down. Stir together the brown sugar and water to make a syrup and pour over slices. Dot with butter. Bake 30 minutes.

Fig Roll Loaf

Makes 1 loaf

When Cynthia Graubart and I found an old
promotional pamphlet produced by White Lily
Flour and leafed through it, one of the things we
found was this recipe. It struck us both as delicious
and enticing, so we made one rather than work
any further. It was, in fact, delicious and enticing.

FILLING

¾ cup dried figs

¼ cup water

¼ cup granulated sugar

1 tablespoon all-purpose flour

¼ teaspoon salt

2 tablespoons lemon juice

DOUGH

2¼ cups all-purpose flour, divided

3 teaspoons baking powder

1 teaspoon salt

2 tablespoons granulated sugar

3 tablespoons chilled shortening,
roughly cut into ½-inch pieces

1 large egg

1 cup milk, divided

Preheat oven to 400 degrees F.

Butter and flour an 8 x 4 x 8-inch loaf pan. Cut out 2 pieces
of parchment or wax paper and fit into the bottom and sides
of the pan. Butter and flour the paper.

Simmer the filling ingredients in a medium saucepan over
medium heat until the figs are soft and begin to break down.
Mash the mixture with a fork until the figs are no longer
lumpy. Set the filling aside to cool.

Fork-sift or whisk 2 cups of the flour with baking powder,
salt, and sugar in a large bowl, preferably wider than it is
deep, and set aside the remaining ¼ cup of flour. Scatter the
butter over the flour and work in by rubbing fingers with the
butter and flour as if snapping thumb and fingers together (or
use two forks or knives, or a pastry cutter) until the mixture
looks like well-crumbled feta cheese, with no piece larger than
a pea. Shake the bowl occasionally to allow the larger pieces
of fat to bounce to the top of the flour, revealing the largest
lumps that still need rubbing. If this method took longer than
5 minutes, place the bowl in the refrigerator for 5 minutes to
rechill the fat.

Make a deep hollow in the center of the flour with the back of your hand. Fork-stir the egg into ⅔ cup milk, reserving ⅓ cup milk; pour the mixture into the hollow and stir with a rubber spatula or large metal spoon, using broad circular strokes to quickly pull the flour into the liquid. Mix just until the dry ingredients are moistened and the sticky dough begins to pull away from the sides of the bowl. If there is some flour remaining on the bottom and sides of the bowl, stir in 1 to 4 tablespoons of reserved milk, just enough to incorporate the remaining flour into the shaggy wettish dough. If the dough is too wet, use more flour when shaping.

Lightly sprinkle a board or other clean surface with some of the reserved flour. Turn the dough out onto the board and sprinkle the top lightly with flour. With floured hands, fold the dough in half, and pat dough out into a ⅓- to ½-inch-thick round, using a little additional flour only if needed. Flour again if necessary and fold the dough in half a second time. Pat dough out into a ½-inch-thick rectangle with one side as long as the bread pan, about 8 inches, using a little additional flour if necessary to keep the dough from sticking to the surface.

Spread the fig filling evenly over the dough. Start from the 8-inch-long side of the roll and roll the dough jelly-roll style using the heel of one hand. Cut across the roll into ¾-inch-wide slices. Stand the slices up in the pan, placing each slice tightly against the last, until the pan is full. Bake for 30 to 35 minutes until a toothpick inserted in the center comes out clean and the loaf is light brown. Remove from oven and cool for 10 minutes on a wire rack. Remove the loaf from the pan, remove the paper, and move carefully to a wire rack to cool completely. Cut the loaf into slices, approximately along the lines created from abutting the sliced dough.

Biscuit Fried Pies

Makes 6 pies

When making biscuits is a regular occurrence, making fried pies is second nature.

FILLING

1 (7-ounce) package dried peaches, figs, or apples, roughly chopped

1 cup water

½ cup granulated sugar

DOUGH

2¼ cups commercial or homemade self-rising flour (page 17), divided

¼ cup chilled shortening or butter, roughly cut into ½-inch pieces

1 cup milk or buttermilk, divided

2 to 4 cups vegetable oil or shortening for frying

Confectioners' sugar for finishing

Put the fruit and water in a medium-size heavy saucepan and let stand for 1 hour or overnight. Cook over low heat until thick enough to cling to a spoon, about 45 minutes. Stir in the sugar.

Fork-sift or whisk 2 cups of flour in a large bowl, preferably wider than it is deep, and set aside the remaining ¼ cup of flour. Scatter the shortening over the flour and work in by rubbing fingers with the shortening and flour as if snapping thumb and fingers together (or use two forks or knives, or a pastry cutter) until the mixture looks like well-crumbled feta cheese, with no piece larger than a pea. Shake the bowl occasionally to allow the larger pieces of fat to bounce to the top of the flour, revealing the largest lumps that still need rubbing. If this method took longer than 5 minutes, place the bowl in the refrigerator for 5 minutes to rechill the fat.

Make a deep hollow in the center of the flour with the back of your hand. Pour ¾ cup of milk or buttermilk into the hollow, reserving ¼ cup, and stir with a rubber spatula or large metal spoon, using broad circular strokes to quickly pull the flour into the milk. Mix just until the dry ingredients are moistened and the sticky dough begins to pull away from the sides of the bowl. If there is some flour remaining on the bottom and sides of the bowl, stir in 1 to 4 tablespoons of reserved milk, just enough to incorporate the remaining flour into the shaggy wettish dough. If the dough is too wet, use more flour when shaping.

Lightly sprinkle a board or other clean surface with some of the reserved flour. Turn the dough out onto the board and sprinkle the top lightly with flour. With floured hands, fold the dough in half, and pat dough out into a round. Pinch off a piece of dough about the size of a small egg. Roll and flatten it into a 5-inch circle. Center about 2 tablespoons of the fruit mixture on the bottom half of the pastry round, about ½ inch from the edge. Fold the top half of the pastry over the fruit, forming a half circle. Trim to within ¼ inch of the filling. Press the edges together with the tines of a fork and prick the top of the pastry in several places. The pies may be made ahead to this point and refrigerated several hours before frying.

When ready to fry, heat enough oil or shortening in a large heavy skillet to reach a depth of ⅛ inch when melted. When the oil is about 325 degrees F, add the pies, prettiest side down. The fat should come about halfway up the pies when all the pies are added. Cook until golden brown. Turn and fry the second side until golden brown, adding more shortening if needed. Drain briefly on a paper towel. Sprinkle with confectioners' sugar, if desired.

VARIATION: Add chopped candied ginger, cinnamon, or pie spices; or substitute brown sugar for the granulated.

VARIATION: SAVORY PIES

These are handy for a picnic. For an apple and sausage fried pie, reduce the amount of apples and add 1 or 2 tablespoons of fried and drained sausage before sealing and frying. For a savory peach fried pie, reduce the amount of peaches and add pepper jelly and a bit of country ham, cut into small strips, before sealing and frying.

Lazy Girl Peach Cobbler

Serves 6 to 8

This batter of self-rising flour, milk, and sugar, which is poured into melted butter and topped with fruit before baking, climbs around the fruit and cobbles on the top as it bakes. The cobbling, named after a cobbled road, denotes a rough and bumpy brown top. Underneath that top is a cake studded with fruit. The edges are crunchy crisp pieces that have soaked in the butter. I love it. The first batter cake recipe I could find in America was printed in the Christian Science Monitor *in the 1920s, but there are allusions to these cakes as early as the 1850s, when baking soda emerged.*

Whether a cobbler is a cakey batter cobbler or a double-crusted pie, it is meant to entice any eater, to embellish memories of home and Southern peaches. As I said, I love it, and the cook will too, as it is easily assembled and baked. If there should be a small amount left, it is a special breakfast treat, cold from the pan or reheated in the microwave.

½ cup butter

1 cup commercial or homemade self-rising flour (page 17)

1 cup light or dark brown sugar

1 cup milk

2 cups sliced fresh or frozen peaches

Preheat oven to 400 degrees F.

Cut the butter in slices and add to a 9 x 13-inch oven-to-table baking dish. Melt on the middle rack of the oven.

Meanwhile, whisk together the flour, sugar, and milk until fairly smooth. Remove the pan with the melted butter from the oven, pour the batter on top of the hot butter, which will sizzle a bit and rise a tad around the outside of the batter. Quickly sprinkle the fruit over the top of the batter and put back in the oven. Bake 40 minutes or until a fork or toothpick inserted in the cake part of the cobbler comes out clean. This may be made ahead, left at room temperature a few hours, or refrigerated or frozen, carefully wrapped. But it is at its very best served hot, straight from the oven.

VARIATION: Serve with ice cream or whipped cream; substitute any soft fruit such as berries, bananas, mangos, and other fruit or any combination; apples and pears need a bit of cooking before they are added to the batter so they may be cooked thoroughly; add candied ginger, cinnamon, chocolate pieces or other favorite flavoring.

Peach Puzzle

Serves 8

This recipe won first place in the Cook's Country lost recipe contest, and I was so intrigued by the idea that the syrup appears in the ramekin, as if by magic, that I have adapted it here.

1 (16-ounce) package frozen sliced peaches, diced, or 6 fresh peaches, peeled and diced

¾ cup packed light or dark brown sugar

6 tablespoons water and/or fruit juice

7 tablespoons chilled butter, divided

½ teaspoon vanilla extract

⅜ teaspoon salt, divided

1½ cups all-purpose flour, divided

2 tablespoons granulated sugar

1 tablespoon baking powder

1 cup milk, divided

Preheat oven to 400 degrees F and position the rack to the middle position.

Place a 6-ounce custard cup or ramekin upside down in the center of a 9-inch pie plate. Arrange the peaches around the ramekin. Combine the brown sugar, water and/or juice, 2 tablespoons of butter, vanilla extract, and ⅛ teaspoon salt in a medium saucepan over medium heat until the sugar dissolves. Pour this sugar mixture over the peaches.

Pulse 1¼ cups of flour, sugar, and baking powder 2 or 3 times in a food processor fitted with the knife or dough blade; set aside the extra ¼ cup of flour. Scatter the remaining butter pieces over the flour mixture and pulse 2 or 3 times until mixture resembles well-crumbled feta cheese, with no piece larger than a pea. Add ¾ cup of milk, reserving ¼ cup, and pulse briefly to incorporate into a shaggy wettish dough. When the blade stops, remove the lid and feel the dough. Add more reserved milk or flour as needed to make a slightly wettish dough. Pulse once or twice more until the dough looks shaggy but together.

Form the dough into a disk shape and roll the dough in a 9-inch circle on a lightly floured work surface. Position the dough over the peaches, enclosing the peaches but not attaching the dough to the pie plate.

Bake for 25 to 30 minutes, until golden brown. Remove from the oven and let cool for 30 minutes. When ready to serve, place a plate over the pie plate and quickly flip the pie plate over. The syrup will miraculously appear in the ramekin, ready for dipping!

Overnight Bananas Foster Biscuit Casserole

Serves 6 to 8

Bananas are best for baking when they are soft enough that no one wants to eat them. My husband frequently complains about their ripening all at one time, but he never complains when I make this dish.

½ cup butter

2 cups light or dark brown sugar

2 cups heavy cream, divided

1 teaspoon vanilla extract

⅛ teaspoon salt

3 bananas, peeled and coarsely smushed

5 cups cut or torn biscuits in ½-inch pieces

3 large eggs

Caramel Sauce (page 181) (optional)

Whipped cream

Preheat oven to 350 degrees F. Melt the butter in a very large heavy saucepan. Stir in the brown sugar and cook, stirring, until the sugar is dissolved. Stir in 1½ cups of cream (reserve ½ cup), vanilla, and salt, continuing to stir until it comes to the boil. Remove from the heat and set aside.

Meanwhile, toss the bananas and biscuit pieces together in a large heavy-duty plastic bag. Beat the eggs with the remaining cream until thoroughly mixed; add to the cooled sugar mixture, whisking continually until thoroughly mixed.

Pour the sugar mixture into the plastic bags and stir it around until the bananas and biscuits are coated. Close the bag and place it in another plastic bag, facing the other way to prevent spills. Refrigerate overnight or at least an hour.

When ready to bake, pour the mixture into a buttered 8-inch round or square, deep cake pan. Make a water bath by placing a clean tea towel in the bottom of a large shallow baking pan. Move the filled cake pan to the tea-towel-lined pan and pour boiling hot water into the pan until the water reaches halfway up the side of the cake pan. Carefully move the water bath with the filled cake pan to the preheated oven. Bake for 45 minutes, until a knife inserted in the center comes out clean and the temperature reaches 200 degrees F. Carefully remove from the oven and water bath. When ready to serve, place under a hot broiler a couple of minutes for a crispy top. Serve with the caramel sauce and whipped cream if desired.

VARIATION: Add ¼ to ⅓ cup rum or bourbon to the brown sugar mixture before adding the egg mixture.

Biscuit Trifle

Serves 6

Layers of pudding and bread are known in most every cuisine. The English have trifle, the Italians have zuppa inglese. *Thank heavens for leftover biscuits for our Biscuit Trifle.*

½ cup lemon juice

Grated rind of 1 lemon, no white attached

¼ cup plus 1 tablespoon granulated sugar

2 large eggs

2 cups heavy cream, divided

12 Rachel's Very Beginner's Cream Biscuits (page 42)

3 cups halved fresh strawberries

Whisk the lemon juice, zest, and ¼ cup sugar together in a small saucepan and bring to a simmer. Whisk the eggs in a separate bowl until they are light and foamy. Slowly pour a little of the lemon mixture into the eggs, whisking as you go. Transfer the eggs into the rest of the lemon mixture and stir for about 5 minutes until the mixture is thick enough to coat the back of a spoon. Pour through a mesh strainer into a bowl and set aside to cool.

Meanwhile, whip 1 cup heavy cream in a separate bowl; fold it into the lemon mixture in three additions, stirring until the custard is smooth.

Whip the additional heavy cream to medium peaks. Slowly add the remaining sugar and beat to incorporate.

Place one biscuit each in the bottom of six clear glasses. Layer ¼ cup of halved strawberries into each glass. Divide half of the lemon custard between the glasses. Repeat with the remaining biscuits, strawberries, and lemon custard. Top each glass with the whipped cream.

Berry-Biscuit Summer Pudding

Serves 4 to 6

In England, summer pudding is made with loaf bread surrounding berries cooked with sugar before being chilled, compressed, and unmolded. Biscuit pudding, a combination of crushed biscuits with the cooked berries and sugar, is equally delicious and equally easy to assemble. I like using a combination of berries, but just one kind may be used. Always taste to be sure of sweetness. It doesn't need whipping cream or ice cream but accommodates them quite happily.

4 to 5 cups fresh berries (blueberries, raspberries, strawberries, blackberries)

1 cup granulated sugar

1 to 2 cups torn or cut biscuits in ½-inch pieces

Cut larger berries such as strawberries into smaller pieces. Add sugar to the prepared berries in a pot that will comfortably hold them. Cover and cook about 10 to 20 minutes over low heat until juices from the berries are extruded. Taste and add more sugar if the berries are too tart. Continue cooking, covered, about 10 minutes more, taking care not to scorch the berries.

Uncover and remove the berries with a slotted spoon, including the juice still clinging to them (approximately 3 cups). Reserve and refrigerate the rest of the juices separately. For each cup of cooked and sweetened berries, add a ½ cup of biscuit pieces, adding more if necessary to make about the consistency of catsup. Stir well until biscuit pieces are not visible.

Line a glass or nonreactive metal bowl (I use a stack bowl like Pyrex) or other mold with plastic wrap. Ladle the mixture into the lined bowl, filling about ⅔ full. Cover the mixture with plastic wrap. Move the bowl to a pie plate or another bowl to catch any drips. Put a heavy can or other weight on top of the wrap over the pudding to compress. Refrigerate several hours or overnight. Remove the weight.

Before serving, remove the plastic wrap from the top
of the pudding. Scoop out any extra juices and add
to the refrigerated reserved juices. Cover the top of
the pudding with a serving plate or dish and carefully
invert the pudding onto the plate or dish over the sink.
Shake the plate or dish slightly if necessary to move the
pudding into position. If the shape needs adjusting, use
the plastic wrap to push the pudding into a rounded
or other pretty shape and then discard wrap. This may
be done ahead several hours or up to a day and kept
refrigerated. It will be pleasant if frozen but not quite
as wonderful. Serve the reserved juices on the side or
spoon over individual plates.

VARIATIONS: Add chopped candied ginger,
cinnamon, mint, or other favorite spices or herbs to
taste before or after cooking berries.

Biscuit Brown Betty

Some form or another of this dessert has been around since colonial times. Made with biscuit crumbs, it is a cross between a bread pudding and a cobbler.

2 cups torn or cut biscuits in 2-inch pieces

½ cup butter, melted

Juice of ½ lemon

½ cup light or dark brown sugar

¾ teaspoon ground cinnamon

½ teaspoon ground ginger

¼ teaspoon ground nutmeg

6 firm-fleshed medium apples, diced

Confectioners' sugar (optional)

Sour cream (optional)

Preheat oven to 375 degrees F.

Spread the biscuit pieces on a rimmed baking sheet and toast for about 8 minutes until golden. Toss in a bowl with the butter. In a separate bowl, whisk together the lemon juice, brown sugar, cinnamon, ginger, and nutmeg. Stir in the apples and toss to coat completely.

Layer half the biscuit pieces over the bottom of an 8-inch square baking pan. Pour the apple mixture over the biscuits, and top with the remaining biscuits. Cover the baking dish entirely with aluminum foil. Bake for 40 minutes until the fruit mixture has softened and has begun to bubble. Remove the foil and bake for 10 minutes more. Allow to cool slightly before serving. Sprinkle with confectioners' sugar and serve with a dollop of sour cream, if desired.

Ginger-Banana Biscuit Bread Pudding

Serves 6

Now that you've undoubtedly made and savored your biscuits, you are still likely to have one or two extras lying around that have gotten a little stale. Rather than throwing them out or slipping one to the dog, this bread pudding is the perfect use for stragglers. The ginger is warm but not too heady, and the creaminess of the banana plays wonderfully with the custard. The pecans add a welcome crunch and help keep this pudding from being too sweet.

4 large eggs

2 cups milk

½ cup light or dark brown sugar

1 teaspoon vanilla extract

¾ teaspoon ground ginger

2 cups torn or cut biscuits in 2-inch pieces

1 banana, sliced

¼ cup chopped pecans, toasted

Butterscotch Sauce (page 180)

Preheat oven to 325 degrees F.

Whisk the eggs together in a medium bowl. Add the milk, brown sugar, vanilla, and ginger; whisk to combine. Toss biscuit pieces, banana slices, and pecans together in a 2-quart soufflé or baking dish. Pour egg mixture over the biscuit mixture. Let the biscuits absorb the liquid for 15 minutes, occasionally pressing down the biscuit pieces to ensure full absorption of the liquid.

When ready to bake, make a water bath by placing a clean tea towel in the bottom of a large shallow baking pan. Move the filled baking dish to the tea-towel-lined pan and pour boiling hot water into the pan until the water reaches halfway up the side of the baking dish. Carefully move the water bath with the baking dish to the preheated oven. Bake for 30 to 40 minutes, until the custard has just set. Serve warm with Butterscotch Sauce drizzled over the pudding.

Cinnamon-Raisin Biscuit Bread Pudding

Serves 6

This bread pudding is the comfort food of childhood. The heady aroma of cinnamon makes it hard to wait for this dish to come out of the oven. As with any casserole, the timing is dependent on the shape of the casserole dish— a deep one will take longer than a shallow one. Whole milk, as in any good pudding or biscuit, is needed.

2 cups torn or cut biscuits in ½-inch pieces

½ cup raisins

2 cups milk

3 large eggs

½ cup light or dark brown sugar

1 teaspoon ground cinnamon

1 teaspoon vanilla extract

½ teaspoon salt

Preheat oven to 350 degrees F.

Grease a 2-quart casserole dish and add the biscuit pieces. Lightly mix in the raisins. Beat the milk and eggs in a separate bowl. Stir in the sugar, cinnamon, vanilla, and salt. Pour the mixture over the biscuit pieces. Let the casserole sit about 30 minutes. (Alternatively, pour the casserole ingredients into a large resealable plastic bag and refrigerate overnight.)

When ready to bake, make a water bath by placing a clean tea towel in the bottom of a large shallow baking pan. Move the filled baking dish to the tea-towel-lined pan and pour boiling hot water into the pan until the water reaches halfway up the side of the baking dish. Carefully move the water bath with the baking dish to the preheated oven. Bake for 50 minutes, until a knife inserted in the center comes out clean.

Water Bath Technique

VARIATION: Bake pudding in 7 or 8 (2-inch) ramekins.

VARIATION: Substitute dried cherries, chopped figs, or dried cranberries for the raisins.

VARIATION: PEAR-GINGER BREAD PUDDING

Substitute ½ cup snipped dried pears for the raisins and 1 tablespoon finely chopped crystallized ginger for the cinnamon.

VARIATION: GINGER BISCUIT BREAD PUDDING

Substitute Julia's Double Ginger Biscuits (page 38) for the regular biscuits. Omit raisins, cinnamon, and vanilla from original recipe. Add 1 teaspoon ground ginger and 2 tablespoons finely chopped candied ginger directly to the biscuit pieces. If you add it to the egg-milk mixture, they will sink to the bottom and not be added evenly to the dish.

VARIATION: COCA-COLA BISCUIT BREAD PUDDING

Use Coca-Cola Biscuits (page 124). Omit raisins and cinnamon from the original recipe. Add ½ cup chocolate chips or chunks. Substitute white sugar for the brown sugar. Add ½ cup cocoa powder to the milk mixture.

Chocolate Soldiers

Makes 20 (1 x 3-inch) fingers

Young children love to dip these treats into a glass of cold milk. Known for decades as chocolate soldiers or chocolate fingers, these strips, served warm from the oven, are a delight for both young and old.

2¼ cups all-purpose flour, divided

3 teaspoons baking powder

1 teaspoon salt

¾ cup granulated sugar

½ cup cocoa powder

¼ cup chilled shortening, roughly cut into ½-inch pieces

1 cup milk, divided

Confectioners' sugar

Preheat oven to 425 degrees F. Grease a baking sheet and set aside.

Fork-sift or whisk 2 cups of flour, baking powder, salt, sugar, and cocoa powder in a large bowl, preferably wider than it is deep, and set aside the remaining ¼ cup of flour. Scatter the shortening over the flour and work in by rubbing fingers with the shortening and flour as if snapping thumb and fingers together (or use two forks or knives, or a pastry cutter) until the mixture looks like well-crumbled feta cheese, with no piece larger than a pea. Shake the bowl occasionally to allow the larger pieces of fat to bounce to the top of the flour, revealing the largest lumps that still need rubbing. If this method took longer than 5 minutes, place the bowl in the refrigerator for 5 minutes to rechill the fat.

Make a deep hollow in the center of the flour with the back of your hand. Pour ⅔ cup of the milk into the hollow, reserving ⅓ cup, and stir with a rubber spatula or large metal spoon, using broad circular strokes to quickly pull the flour into the milk. Mix just until the dry ingredients are moistened and the sticky dough begins to pull away from the sides of the bowl. If there is some flour remaining on the bottom and sides of the bowl, stir in 1 to 4 tablespoons of reserved milk, just enough to incorporate the remaining flour into the shaggy wettish dough. If the dough is too wet, use more flour when shaping.

Lightly sprinkle a board or other clean surface with some of the reserved flour. Turn the dough out onto the board and sprinkle the top lightly with flour. With floured hands, fold the dough in half, and pat dough out into a ⅓- to ½-inch-thick round, using a little additional flour only if needed. Flour again if necessary, and fold the dough in half a second time. If the dough is still clumpy, pat and fold a third time. Pat dough out into a ½-inch-thick round. Brush off any visible flour from the top. Cut dough into 1 x 3-inch strips using a pastry wheel or knife.

Using a metal spatula if necessary, move the strips to the pan or baking sheet. Bake the strips on the top rack of the oven for a total of 12 to 15 minutes, depending on thickness, until light golden brown. After 6 minutes, rotate the pan in the oven so that the front of the pan is now turned to the back, and check to see if the bottoms are browning too quickly. If so, slide another baking pan underneath to add insulation and retard browning. Continue baking another 6 to 9 minutes until the strips are light golden brown. When the strips are done, remove from the oven and sprinkle with confectioners' sugar.

Bibliography

Baking Illustrated. Brookline, MA: America's Test Kitchen, 2004.

Beard, James. *James Beard's American Cookery*. Boston: Little, Brown, 1972.

Better Homes and Gardens Cookbook. Des Moines, IA: Better Homes and Gardens, Meredith Publish Co., 1950.

Charleston Receipts. Charleston, SC: The League, 1950.

Claiborne, Craig. *Craig Claiborne's Southern Cooking*. New York: Times Books, 1987.

Corriher, Shirley O. *BakeWise: The Hows and Whys of Successful Baking with Over 200 Magnificent Recipes*. New York: Scribner, 2008.

Dabney, Joseph Earl. *Smokehouse Ham, Spoon Bread & Scuppernong Wine*. Nashville, TN: Cumberland House, 1998.

Dull, Mrs. S. R. *Southern Cooking*. Atlanta: The Ruralist Press, 1928.

Dupree, Nathalie. *Cooking of the South*. New York: Irena Chalmers Cookbooks, 1982.

———. *Nathalie Dupree Cooks Everyday Meals from a Well-Stocked Pantry*. New York: Clarkson Potter, 1995. Print.

———. *Nathalie Dupree Cooks Quick Meals for Busy Days*. New York: Clarkson Potter, 1996.

———. *Nathalie Dupree's Comfortable Entertaining*. New York: Viking, 1998.

———. *Nathalie Dupree's Matters of Taste*. New York: Knopf, 1990.

———. *Nathalie Dupree's Shrimp & Grits*. Layton, UT: Gibbs Smith, Publisher, 2006.

Fowler, Damon Lee. *Dining at Monticello: In Good Taste and Abundance*. Charlottesville, VA: Thomas Jefferson Foundation, 2005.

———. *Damon Lee Fowler's New Southern Baking: Classic Flavors for Today's Cook*. New York: Simon & Schuster, 2005.

The Good Housekeeping Cookbook. New York: Rinehart and Company, 1944.

King, Daisy. *Miss Daisy's Healthy Southern Cooking*. Nashville, TN: Cumberland House, 2004.

A Lady Of Charleston and Sarah Rutledge. *The Carolina Housewife or, House and Home*. Charleston, SC: W. R. Babcock, 1851.

Lewis, Edna, and Mary Goodbody. *In Pursuit of Flavor*. New York: Knopf, 1988.

———. *The Taste of Country Cooking*. New York: Knopf, 1976.

Neal, Bill. *Bill Neal's Southern Cooking*. Chapel Hill: University of North Carolina Press, 1985.

Payne, Susan Carlisle. *The Southern Living Cookbook*. Birmingham, AL: Oxmoor House, 1987.

Peterson, James. *Baking*. Berkeley: Ten Speed Press, 2009.

Randolph, Mary, Henry Stone, and Henry Stone. *The Virginia house-wife: Method is the soul of management*, second edition, with amendments and additions. Washington [DC]: Printed by Way & Gideon, Ninth Street, near Pennsylvania Avenue, 1825.

Rhett, Blanche Salley, and Lettie Gay. *200 Years of Charleston Cooking*. New York: H. Smith & R. Haas, 1934.

Robinson, Sallie Ann., and Gregory Wrenn. Smith. *Gullah Home Cooking the Daufuskie Way*. Chapel Hill: The University of North Carolina, 2003.

Rombauer, Irma Von Starkloff, and Marion Rombauer Becker. *Joy of Cooking*. Indianapolis: Bobbs-Merrill, 1946, 1964.

Ruhlman, Michael. *Ratio: The Simple Codes Behind the Craft of Everyday Cooking*. New York: Scribner, 2009.

Smalls, Alexander, and Hettie Jones. *Grace the Table: Stories and Recipes from My Southern Revival*. New York: Harper Collins Publishers, 1997.

Smith, E. *The compleat housewife, or, accomplish'd gentlewoman's companion*. London: Printed for J. Pemberton, 1729.

Taylor, John Martin. *The New Southern Cook: Two Hundred Recipes from the South's Best Chefs and Home Cooks*. New York: Bantam Books, 1995.

Villas, James, with Martha Pearl Villas. *My Mother's Southern Desserts*. New York: Morrow, 1998.

Index

METRIC CONVERSION CHART

Volume Measurements		Weight Measurements		Temperature Conversion	
U.S.	**Metric**	**U.S.**	**Metric**	**Fahrenheit**	**Celsius**
1 teaspoon	5 ml	½ ounce	15 g	250	120
1 tablespoon	15 ml	1 ounce	30 g	300	150
¼ cup	60 ml	3 ounces	90 g	325	160
⅓ cup	75 ml	4 ounces	115 g	350	180
½ cup	125 ml	8 ounces	225 g	375	190
⅔ cup	150 ml	12 ounces	350 g	400	200
¾ cup	175 ml	1 pound	450 g	425	220
1 cup	250 ml	2¼ pounds	1 kg	450	230

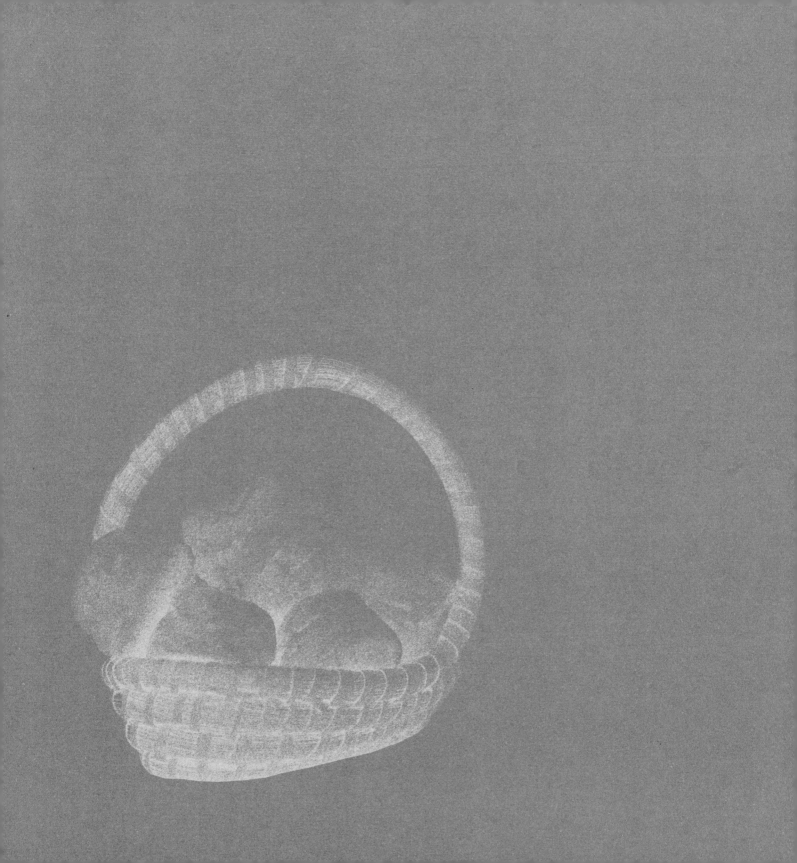